THE BINGE CODE

7 Unconventional Keys to End Binge Eating & Lose Excess Weight

ALISON C KERR

Contributor: RICHARD KERR

Contributor: GEORGIA KEIGHERY

Contributor: CATHERINE LIBERTY

Dear binge eating,

Let's break up.

ツ

Contents

ACKNOWLEDGEMENTS

I want to acknowledge YOU, the reader.

For the imperfect, flawed, quirky, beautiful, wonderful person that you are.

I wrote this for you.

Legal Disclaimer

This book is not intended as a substitute for the medical advice of physicians. The reader should regularly consult a physician in matters relating to his/her health and particularly with respect to any symptoms that may require diagnosis or medical attention.

The information provided in this book is designed to provide helpful information on the subjects discussed. This book is not meant to be used, nor should it be used, to diagnose or treat any medical condition. For diagnosis or treatment of any medical problem, consult your own physician. The publisher and author are not responsible for any specific health or allergy needs that may require medical supervision and are not liable for any damages nor negative consequences from any treatment, action, application or preparation, to any person reading or following the information in this book. This book is sold with the understanding that the publisher is not engaged to render any type of psychological, medical, legal, or any other kind of professional advice.

Any recommendations described within should be tried only under the guidance of a licensed health-care practitioner. The author and publisher assume no responsibility for any outcome of the use of this book in self treatment or under the care of a licensed practitioner.

MORE THAN JUST A BOOK

The Binge Code is more than just a book. It's a complete program that comes with a range of bonus tools and support materials, including:

- 5 powerful guided meditations (to help you overcome binge eating faster)
- The Binge Code food journal
- The Binge Code cheat sheet
- A binge tracker
- A daily checklist
- An active support community

 You can access all these from www.thebingecode.com/bonus

THIS BOOK SHOULD NOT EXIST

Fifteen years ago, this book couldn't exist. Fifteen years ago, I wasn't sure if tomorrow would exist.

I was going to die soon. It was inevitable. There's only so much abuse a body can take. I'd been bingeing and purging food for over 10 years at that point, usually 10 times a day and it felt like all the years of self-inflicted damage were finally catching up with me.

I'd lost my menstrual cycle, I'd become socially withdrawn and depressed. I was suffering from weight fluctuations, panic attacks, heart palpitations, bad teeth, severe food obsession and body preoccupation. My life was an endless cycle of bingeing, purging, then starving, bingeing, purging, then starving. Food was a battle ground and hunger was my enemy. Normal life felt like a distant forgotten memory.

In 2003 I hit rock bottom. I found myself passed out on the toilet floor. My heart was palpitating, I felt shaky, weak, broken and I instinctively knew that my body wouldn't allow me to carry on this way for much longer. I had abused it enough. There was a limit and I had reached mine. This had to stop. I didn't want to die. With nothing left to lose I decided that I was going to dedicate my life to defeating this.

The idea that I could:

- ever stop bingeing,
- help thousands of other people to stop bingeing,
- write a book about stopping bingeing, and
- appreciate the insight and understanding my suffering gave me…

Well, that was just an impossible dream.

It wasn't like I didn't try to stop. Oh my, I tried so hard to stop. With every atom of my being, with every ounce of my willpower, I tried to resist the urge to binge on food but it never worked. I couldn't stop. I wasn't sure if I was mad, broken, lacked willpower or all of the above. What I did know was that I was terrified, alone, ill and that my life was in danger.

Perhaps most dangerous of all was the fact that I was beginning to lose hope. Hope of ever recovering. Hope of ever being free. Living without hope is a dark place to be.

So, right off the bat, I want to give you hope. More than anything I want to give you hope.

If you suffer from binge eating you know how much control food can hold over your life. Every second of every day you are bombarded by thoughts of food. Every food advert, fast food joint, convenience store and vending machine can trigger uncontrollable food cravings. Food is everywhere, all the time and it's exhausting.

Eating food fills you simultaneously with feelings of pleasure, guilt, dread and shame. Somehow you can just eat, eat and eat and never seem to reach the point where you feel satisfied. Afterwards you worry about weight gain and berate yourself for lacking control. In the back of your mind you fear that it is too late for you, that you are too weak, too broken and you worry that you are doomed to suffer with the pain and misery of life as a binge eater.

I can tell you right now that these fears are unfounded. From the diversity of people and success stories I have witnessed over the past decade, I can tell you without a doubt that no one is beyond help and **that there is no such thing as being too weak or too broken** to break free from binge eating. You can get your life back. A life completely free from any urge to eat vast quantities of food.

So if you're wondering if this book is for you, here's what you need to know.

In this book I am going to show you exactly how to overcome your binge eating issues, make peace with food and achieve your optimal, natural weight without dieting.

I've been coaching sufferers of bulimia and binge eating since 2007. I published my first book "The Bulimia Help Method" through Amazon.com in 2014. It is now the best reviewed bulimia recovery book on Amazon. This book uses some of the same core principles and ideas but they have been specifically tailored towards binge eaters.

It doesn't matter if you binge on food once a week or multiple times a day. It doesn't matter if you are overweight, underweight or normal weight. If you find yourself uncontrollable around food, you are in the right place, this book will help you, this book is your blueprint for success. Trust me, you can get over this, you are not doomed, this is not a life sentence, **you can have hope**.

YOU ARE TRAPPED

I remember it well. It was early in the morning, I had just woken up, the sun was shining through the curtains. I had just finished University and I was feeling good about myself. As I lay in bed I made a decision there and then. Enough was enough. Today was the day. No matter what, I was **not** going to binge on food. I felt absolutely 100% determined. I was going to do it. Nothing was going to stop me. I was going to use every ounce of my willpower, determination and strength. I felt confident. I felt empowered. I felt like I was ready to take it on.

4 hours. I lasted 4 miserable hours.

I felt devastated. What was wrong with me? Why couldn't I just stop myself? Where was my willpower?

I honestly believed that if I held out long enough and ignored the urge to binge it would just disappear.

And that was it. Right there. The most common mistake people make when they are attempting to overcome binge eating. Relying solely on willpower. So, off the bat, **I want to tell you there is nothing wrong with your willpower**. Your willpower is fine. Perfectly normal.

The problem is that you are trapped. Your body, mind and emotions have become **trapped** in a continual cycle of bingeing on food. Until you break free the trap, binge urges **will always remain**. They'll never go away. Eventually your willpower to resist the urge runs out.

Imagine you're caught in a rope trap. It wouldn't matter how much you struggled and tried to escape, until the ropes were untied you would always remain trapped. It's not a matter of you just "wanting to escape enough", you need to be physically released before you can be free.

Think of your willpower like a battery pack. It's good for short term goals and general motivation. No one has enough willpower to continually resist the urge to binge forever. Eventually, no matter how determined you are, **if the urge is there, you will give in**. This is the reason why your most fervent promises to stop bingeing, made in the heat of post-binge shame and exasperation, so often fail.

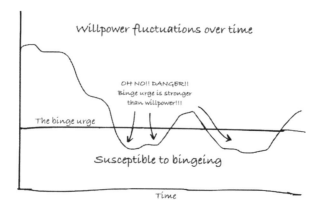

So, stop berating yourself for a lack of willpower or a lack of strength and determination. **You have ample willpower, ample strength and ample determination**. In fact, we are going to tap into that wonderful willpower, strength and determination of yours and use it break free from binge eating forever.

———

SO, WHAT'S IN THIS BOOK?

PART 1 OF THE BINGE CODE: ZEN10 YOUR BINGE URGES

To begin with I am going to teach you a powerful technique you can use to tackle any binge urges or cravings. I call this the Zen10 technique. This won't get rid of the cravings completely but it will dramatically reduce their intensity and power over you.

You can then keep the Zen10 technique in your back pocket, ready to use as you progress through the rest of the program.

PART 2 OF THE BINGE CODE: BREAK FREE FROM THE BINGE TRAPS

Do you ever feel trapped in a cycle of binge eating? Perhaps the reason you feel trapped is because you are trapped! Over the past ten years working with binge eaters, I have identified seven traps that hold people in a continual cycle of bingeing on food. I call these 'the binge traps'.

The binge traps are a prison that hold us trapped in a cycle of binge eating, emotional eating and food obsession. They make us feel guilty and ashamed about what we have eaten. They make us feel powerless and weak around food and they keep us stressed, emotionally drained and overweight.

In part two of this book we are going to explore the seven different binge traps. We are going to examine how each trap works and then I am going to give you the keys to break free from each one. Seven keys to unlock the seven binge traps. Once you unlock all seven traps you won't have any more binge urges, you will notice a dramatic improvement in your wellbeing and **you will be completely free**.

The seven binge traps are:

1. The Diet Trap
2. The Yo-Yo Blood Sugar Trap

3. The Nutritional Deficiency Trap
4. The Habit Trap
5. The Food Rules Trap
6. The False Friend Trap
7. The Inner Critic Trap

If you binge on food, chances are all seven traps will apply to you. Some traps may be more relevant to you than others but I'm pretty confident that you will find elements in each that you can relate to.

PART 3 OF THE BINGE CODE: BIOBALANCING™

After you break free from the binge traps, I am going to teach you the art of **BioBalancing™**.

There are two ways you can choose to manage your weight. The painful way and the painless way. You're probably pretty familiar with the painful way. You know the one; continual diets, food deprivation, bingeing on food, weight fluctuations, negative self-talk and generally feeling miserable.

However there is another way, an effortless, painless way, with no restriction, no diets, no deprivation, no weight fluctuations. This involves learning, understanding and responding to your own individual needs so that you eat the right amount of food that is perfect for you. I call this **BioBalancing™** and it's life changing in the best possible way.

BioBalancing™ is really the art of maintaining **balance**. Right now, you are very much off-balance. The kind of appetite you have now, the cravings for all kinds of foods, binge urges, holding on to excess weight, all of this is your body's way of communicating with you that you're off-balance.

To get back in balance we first have to navigate our way out of the seven binge traps. In doing so we help to balance our body, mind and emotions. Finally, BioBalancing™ will enable you to comfortably maintain a state of balance. A balanced body does not want to hold on to any excess weight. A balanced body does not want to binge on food. By staying in balance you make sure you never again fall back into the binge traps.

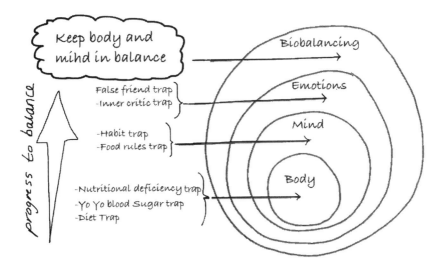

So that's it. That's the road map ahead. I hope you are feeling excited to go on this journey with me. I will be with you every step of the way, providing you with tips, tools and strategies to help supercharge your journey to binge freedom.

That's the thing when it comes to overcoming binge eating. For most people it's not just one thing. One tool or technique doesn't cut the mustard. It's not a one size fits all. That's why The Binge Code is a series of steps and techniques. It's a broad spectrum of strategies that work well together and bring your body back into balance.

But before we start applying the Binge Code to your life, let's take a few chapters to cover some things I really want you to know…

Your life after binge eating

The Binge Code is not a quick fix (sadly they do not exist). Stopping binge eating does require some commitment and perseverance. I would love to click my fingers and miraculously cure you of all eating issues, but the reality is that it takes a little longer than that. For some of you it may take 2-6 months before the binge urge really dissipates. Yes, I know some of you will be disappointed by this fact, but the fact is that it takes time to break free from the binge traps (especially if you have been bingeing on food for a number of years). A little bit of patience is required. The good news is that as you progress, binge cravings will become increasingly less intense and less frequent. From now on it's only going to get easier.

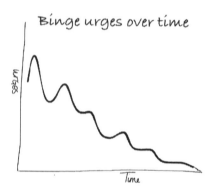

One of the biggest fears for many is 'the void'. The idea that once binge eating has been removed from your life, all that's left will be a gaping dark hole. But in reality, there is no void. The space left when binge eating is removed is replaced with something entirely wonderful... you! Your sense of self, your personality. You'll discover the imperfect, flawed, quirky, beautiful, wonderful person that you are.

This doesn't happen overnight. It's a gradual process as you slowly discover the wonderful things about this new version of you. I will never forget the time I discovered my old laugh. A few months after I stopped bingeing my husband told me one of his rather silly jokes, but it made me laugh really hard, a proper, huge, belly laugh. It was wonderful. I hadn't laughed like that in years and I had forgotten that I used to do it all the time before binge eating took over my life.

That's the thing about the process of healing from binge eating. As you start to take care of yourself you start to come alive again. It's like a fog lifts to reveal all these living, vibrant parts of you that have been trodden down. It's like being plugged back in, or coming out of a coma and as you wake up and come alive you get to know yourself again. After removing binge eating from my life I realized that I am deeply sensitive, that I'm playful and that I have a great sense of humor.

In Japan there's an ancient technique of repairing objects called Kintsugi. It's the art of repairing broken ceramic bowls instead of discarding them. They fill the cracks with a gold speckled resin so that when the bowl is repaired it's even more beautiful and valuable than before.

Your binge eating issues are the cracks through which you can become an even more amazing person. Once you overcome binge eating, your experience can have a positive meaning and purpose in your life.

Famous Psychiatrist Elisabeth Kübler-Ross wrote: "The most amazing people we have known are those who have known defeat, known suffering, known struggle, known loss and have found their way out of the depths. These people have an appreciation, a sensitivity and an understanding of life that fills them with compassion, gentleness and a deep loving concern. **Amazing people do not just happen.**"

LOSING EXCESS WEIGHT

L et's talk about your weight. Specifically let's take a moment to discuss what you can expect to happen to your weight when you follow the Binge Code.

If you have been bingeing on food for an extended period of time it may have lead to unnecessary weight gain. By following the Binge Code you can expect your body to release any excess weight and eventually settle at it's natural set point weight. At your set point you will find that your weight will be much more stable and easy to maintain.

Any excess weight you lose following the Binge Code will come off gradually. You will need to have a little patience here. It won't be anything like the weight-loss you may have experienced in the past. You may experience some weight fluctuations. Some weeks there may be a slight weight gain and other weeks a slight weight loss, but, in general if you look at the big picture you will see an overall pattern of weight loss towards your set point.

Patience is important here. You must give your body time and space to heal and rebalance. I would suggest giving this process at least six months to unfold. Six months is such a small amount of time compared to a lifetime free from binge eating.

Following this program, if you are within the "normal" weight range for your height and build then chances are that you will end up at a very similar weight once your body finds its natural set point. If you are underweight, you may need to be prepared to gain some "required" weight.

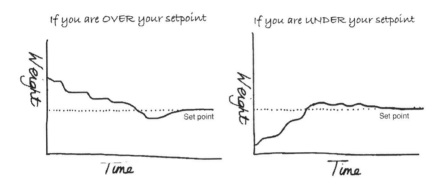

So what is your "set point"?

We are all made in **different shapes and sizes**. Several studies have shown that for adults who do not consciously try to control their body size, weight is remarkably stable over time. This is your "set point" – a reference point around which the body tries to keep weight stable.

Our set point has a range that can swing between 5-10 lbs throughout our lives. Within this range, weight is relatively easy to modify through lifestyle changes. Some of us have a heavier set point, some of us have a lighter set point, but most of us are somewhere in between. Set point is different for everyone and can be different for people of the same height. A very thin person may appear underweight but this might be their natural set point.

Genetics play a big part as to where body fat is distributed, how big your bones are, how big your muscles are, etc. You can't work out or starve your way to changing your genetics. Keeping your body weight below its set point range, even for years, does not lead the body to regard the thinner state as the new norm. Your body will continue to resist the new weight and fight to get back to it's comfort zone (Keesey 1993). Women and men who attempt to achieve this particular body type (but lack the genetic material to do so) are setting themselves up for a lifetime of yo-yo dieting, weight fluctuations, binge eating.

Set points tend to increase with age, by about half a kilogram a year, especially in people who don't exercise enough. A diet very high in fat and sugar and the presence of dieting in general, seem to promote a higher set point. Regular (healthy and appropriate) exercise can result in a lower set-point.

If you have been struggling with food restriction and weight issues for many years it can be difficult to determine your set point. Observing your weight patterns over time gives an indication of what your natural weight may be. If your weight has gone up and down dramatically then your set point is probably somewhere in the middle.

To further determine your set point, ask yourself: what kind of bone structure and body shape does your mother have? What about your father? Other family members? Remember that the weight of your relatives isn't the point of reference here - they may have their own dietary complications at play. It's more about their skeletal frame and general shape.

To be truly free from binge eating you must accept and embrace your natural set point weight. Consider this: only about 5% of American women have the ultra-long and thin body type that is seen almost exclusively in the media. It also helps to remember that the majority of the images you see in the media have been heavily edited, digitally retouched, stretched and airbrushed. It is an illusion, it is not reality.

The only way for **life-long happiness** with food is to live at your ideal, natural, healthy weight. By doing this you will feel stronger, fitter and better than you have ever felt the entire time you binge ate.

PART 1

ZEN10 YOUR BINGE URGES

UNDERSTANDING BINGE URGES

I still clearly remember the onset of an overwhelming binge urge. It would seem to appear from nowhere. It would just materialize out of the blue and then I was in the urge. It was happening already and I hadn't even seen it coming. I just suddenly wanted to, needed to eat. And when I say eat, I mean eat everything.

Following the Binge Code, it usually takes 2-6 months for your binge urges to completely disappear. So, in the mean time I want to give you a tool you can use against any urges that may arise. It is called the Zen10 technique and it will help you to resist acting on any urges. You may experience a binge urge, but you won't feel so compelled to give into it. It will ease the intensity of those binge urges and make them much more manageable. Eventually with time, following the program your urges will disappear completely.

The first thing we need to do though, is to learn a little more about binge urges.

So, what is a binge "urge"?

Understanding this concept is fundamental to breaking free from binge eating.

Imagine you're alone, bored and feeling down. You've have a stressful day and there is food in the cupboard but strangely you have absolutely no urge or desire to binge on it. Would you binge? I'm guessing not. That would be like drinking 5 gallons of water even though you had no thirst or urge to do so. The point here is this: If you didn't experience an urge to binge, you wouldn't binge.

It is the "urge" or "craving" to binge that makes you binge. Our goal isn't just to stop you from bingeing, it is to completely remove the urge and desire to do so. This is an important distinction because by removing the urge to binge we help to ensure lifelong freedom.

Some binge eating treatment methods teach you strategies to manage urges to binge. For example, some programs encourage lifelong avoidance of potential trigger foods. The problem with this approach is that even though you may not be bingeing you will continue to have a deep-seated fear of food. You will not be free. I would not call this true recovery, it is only maintenance.

So let's learn a little more about the binge urge. Why is it so hard to resist the binge urge? Why is it so powerful? Why does it make us feel so powerless?

To help answer some of those questions let's run through what actually happens whenever you experience a binge urge and why it can be so challenging to resist.

———

HOW AN URGE LEADS TO A BINGE

You experience a strong urge to binge on food.

This is generally a random, powerful urge to consume vast quantities of food.

You have a strong emotional response to the urge.

You may panic in response to the binge urge: "Oh no! here comes a binge. Why am I feeling this way? What is wrong with me?".

Or, if you already know that you are going to give yourself permission to binge on food, you may react to the binge urge with excitement. You're finally going to allow yourself to eat!

"Well, it's going to happen. I can finally have the release of a binge! I can just let go and have all the bad foods I've been craving."

Or, it could be both panic and excitement. Part of your mind wants to binge and part of your mind doesn't: "Just this one last time! I'll make it extra big - the final binge - and then I'll never do it again."

Your fight-or-flight response kicks in.

These intense emotional responses instantly **send your body into fight-or-flight mode**. Fight-or-flight is a biological response that has evolved to protect us from danger. Your body and brain don't know the difference between an actual threat, such as being stalked by an animal that's about to kill you and a perceived threat, like facing an emotionally extreme situation. They're the same thing as far as your physiology is concerned and they induce the same response.

Your body kicks into high gear by releasing hormones like adrenalin and cortisol. These chemicals surge through your body, increasing your heart rate and breathing, tensing your muscles and constricting your blood vessels. You feel jittery, on edge, anxious, even excited.

Fight-or-flight intensifies the need to respond to the binge urge.

The incredible intensity of the fight-or-flight response is designed to provoke an extreme emotional reaction to make you act immediately. Millions of years of evolution have made it this way for good reason. If a lion jumped out at you in the jungle you can bet you would want to respond quickly. It's an instinctive response. **You feel you must react** to the stress trigger **immediately to survive**. It's the same with your need to respond to the binge urge. You brain is telling you it must be dealt with. **NOW!**

Your cravings for energy-dense foods increase.

In fight-or-flight mode the body uses up an enormous amount of energy as your physiology goes into overdrive. This sparks the release of a group of hormones called glucocorticoids. The role of glucocorticoids is to replenish that lost energy by spiking your cravings for sugar and energy-dense foods and storing fat in your abdomen, to ensure that you have enough fuel to survive future threats (so you can keep running from that lion). **This intensifies your cravings even further** and these hormones stick around in your blood even after the threat is removed.

Your brain goes into autopilot as you lose the ability to think logically or clearly.

The part of your brain that's essential for the experience of emotions and perception is called the amygdala. During fight-or-flight the amygdala gets hijacked. It's overrun in a neurochemical process that **disables your capacity to access the part of your brain responsible for rational thought (your neocortex)**. This is why it's nearly impossible to think through the situation with calm logic. If you're in front of that lion, your brain doesn't want you to stop to remember the great plans you made about how to deal with this logically - it just wants you to run! The space to weigh up pros and cons, where you consider your options, is eliminated and **you find yourself reacting automatically, without thinking about it**.

"When you start binge eating it's almost as if you turn into a robot and you are in autopilot and you remember everything you read and how you shouldn't be doing that but it's like at that moment you suddenly stop caring and the most important thing to you at that point is stuffing your face with food." - Clara T

You cannot control this binge urge and this leads to *more* fear.

In reality you have very little control over how the urge to binge makes you feel, how long it stays, or how intense it is. Yet you may try your very best to control it.

You could try yelling at the binge urge, screaming at it to go away, but it won't. You could try presenting the most compelling and logical arguments in the world against a binge urge, but still this doesn't work. These things do not work because a binge urge **doesn't respond to logic or emotion**.

Realizing you cannot control the binge urge can make you feel even more weak and powerless against it. So, what happens? More panic, more fear, more stress. The fight-or-flight cycle spirals around again. The lions keep coming!

You blame yourself.

At this point you blame yourself. You think the fault is in your lack of willpower, your emotional weakness, or your defective personality. This perpetuates the feelings of powerlessness and defeat and makes you feel even worse.

The only way you know to numb this feeling is to BINGE!

You don't know any other way to deal with these intense emotions. Helplessness, hopelessness, fear, anger, anxiety, self-loathing and that feeling of being unable to escape. You haven't developed any other method for coping with seemingly unbearable feelings like these other than bingeing.

So, you give in and binge.

As you can see a binge urge is actually a cascading avalanche of emotions, cravings, chemical responses and biological reflexes. It's a lot to deal with and it can all happen in a matter of seconds. No wonder you've found it so hard to resist your binge urges.

You may be thinking, "Well then HOW am I EVER going to escape my binge urge if I have no control over it? I'm doomed!".

Don't worry, you are far from doomed. I just wanted to give you a brief overview of the process. I know it can feel a little overwhelming to begin with, but now I want to show you a powerful technique you can use to reduce the intensity of any urges. I call it the Zen10 technique.

This is a technique I have developed over 10 years of working with binge eating sufferers. However, I want you to keep in mind that the Zen10 technique will not get rid of your binge urges completely (we need to escape from the binge traps to do that), but it will make those urges much more manageable and allow you to feel much more in control. Think of it as a temporary band aid, a helpful solution until the underlying issues have been resolved.

SPOTTING A BINGE URGE

The first thing we need to do is to spot a binge urge. Noticing is the key. If you notice what's happening, then you can make a choice about how you respond to what's happening. You can choose to **do something else rather than reacting with your usual, habitual patterns**. You can interrupt your conditioned response. You can apply the Zen10 technique.

First, we've got to catch a binge urge sneaking up so that we have time to stop it in its tracks. In order to do this we must first recognize the initial binge urge signs.

Some early physical indications of an oncoming binge urge might be:

- Feeling physically jittery and agitated
- Feeling tight or heavy in your chest
- Feeling flustered and constricted in your throat
- Shallow, quick breathing
- Churning in your stomach
- Feeling disconnected from your body (not being able to feel your body clearly)
- Not being able to settle physically

Early emotional indications could include:

- Sudden anger
- Blurry thinking
- Emotional unease
- A sense of sadness out of nowhere
- Feeling uncomfortable in your own skin
- Being annoyed at yourself or the world
- Feeling frustrated or having lots of chaotic thoughts

Perhaps certain thoughts appear as precursors, like:

- "Agh! this is hopeless!"
- "I'm too tired to keep going."
- "I've blown it!"
- "That's it - I give up!"
- "I'll never be able to sustain this."

Think about what your signs may be. How do your behaviors change when you're on the verge of a binge? How do you start acting when you're feeling out of control around food? What are the signs that show you're struggling? Are you very quiet? Do you exhibit nervous behaviors like nail picking, hair twisting or hand rubbing? Try to make a note of the signs, no matter how small. This is valuable information. Binge urge sensations are different for everyone and learning your specific cues gives you the power to gain the upper hand.

THE ZEN10 TECHNIQUE

As we've seen previously, a binge urge triggers our fight or flight response which then floods our body with chemicals, shuts down our brain and intensifies cravings for fatty, sugary foods. This can turn us into brainless, food eating zombies. We need to snap out of it somehow. We need to do something sudden and unexpected to totally defy the habitual thought patterns, **break free from autopilot** and take us out of fight-or-flight.

Whenever you notice you're craving a binge, in that moment, I want you to say to yourself, **"Zen10!"**. So that the phrase "Zen10!" reminds you that you're going to do something different this time. **This will help snap you out of autopilot.**

Then give yourself 10 minutes before acting on your urges. By giving yourself a buffer of 10 minutes you help to create a space between your binge urges and your response. In that space you allow the binge urge to rise and fall and **do whatever it wishes**, but you take no action towards having a binge.

10 minutes is a short, manageable length of time. If you try to hold off any longer you may feel overwhelmed, deprived or unable to cope. Set your watch if you need to and simply avoid taking any action towards a binge urge until the 10 minutes have passed.

Research by neuroscientists proves that even a 10-minute wait can **drastically reduce** the brain's response to a craving. Binge urges are not constant. They ebb and flow in waves. By delaying 10 minutes you give yourself the opportunity to see if the urge will pass. This is especially true if the binge urge triggered your fight-or-flight response. It may take a good ten minutes (or longer) for you to start to feel normal again as your body needs time to flush out all the stress hormones that were activated.

Resting in the space between

Once you have allocated your 10 minutes the next step is to cultivate a space between your cravings and your reaction.

Have you ever seen zen monk meditating? They can sit still for hours at a time. They may experience periods of feeling uncomfortable, they may feel itchy, a fly might land on their nose, but they still don't move. They are able to shrug off any discomfort and place it aside. Their mind is able to remain strong, resilient and zen like. They don't react to their impulses. There is a still space between their impulses and their actions.

We can do something similar. We often react to binge urges without thinking. We frequently don't choose our behaviors so much as just act them out. But we can learn from our zen monk friends. We can cultivate **a space between an urge and our response**.

When we have a powerful binge urge it can feel like it's coming from deep inside our core. It feels really personal, like it's a part of who we are. It can feel like a response to some unmet emotional need, or a response to some past trauma or pain. Even though it feels personal, we can still separate our personal self from it. We don't need to respond to it instantly. We don't need to be so reactive. Instead, we can learn to notice that there is a "**space**" before we react. We can learn to make use of this "space". Within that moment of space we can **observe** without judgment, we can **accept** that we are triggered and then we can ultimately choose how to respond to the trigger. This puts us back in the driving seat and in control.

Zen10...

"Between stimulus and response there is a space. In that space is our power to choose our response. In our response lies our growth and our freedom."

Viktor E. Frankl

Being aware of that freedom and that space is half the battle. When you're in the throes of a binge urge, the waves engulf you and you can't think about anything else. So here are some useful techniques to help cultivate a sense of space.

Realize that you are in control.

The binge urges do not control you. **You are in control.** Yes, I know in the middle of a binge urge it can feel impossible to resist. But even the most powerful desires are just **feelings-coated information.** They are simply messages, suggestions that can be followed or ignored. We can choose our reaction.

For example, should you find yourself going towards the fridge for a binge, the very moment you notice your body reacting with movement... stop moving. Stand completely still. Realize that your thoughts cannot make you move. Realize your body is totally unaffected. The urge to binge is powerless unless you act on it. You may feel waves or a compulsion to binge, but they cannot make you move. You have the power. You are not your thoughts, you are not your desires. You are the **strong silent one** underneath it all. The zen one.

The Zen Tree

Visualization is a really powerful tool here. One I like to use is to visualize yourself as a strong oak tree and the binge urges are the wind blowing against the leaves. No matter how strong the wind is the tree does not topple or fall over. Its roots grow strong and deep. It stands tall and proud.

Sure, a strong wind may cause the tree to bend a little, or sway from side to side. That's okay. The tree doesn't mind. It's not bothered. It doesn't stand rigid, fight back or resist. The wind can do as it pleases.

The tree just accepts the flow and ebb of the wind. In time the wind will calm, the storm will pass and the tree remains strong.

Imagine yourself like a tall tree. You are strong. Feel your roots go deep into the earth. Feel your branches reaching upwards towards the sky. Let the binge urge wind blow all it wants. Let it rustle your leaves, know that you are strong and that you can weather any storm.

Another visualization technique that my clients like to use is the protective bubble visualization.

Imagine you are surrounded by a protective bubble. The bubble fills you with protective energy. A pure white light. Feel it as it enters your body filling you from your feet to your head. Feel it as it rises up. Feel it strengthen your resolve, strengthen your resilience, strengthen your zen mind.

Play around here and find a visualization technique that works for you.

"The binge urge brought up images for me of an old music video by Fiona Apple. The original song 'Across the Universe' was written by John Lennon and Paul McCartney. In Fiona Apple's video for the cover song there is mass chaos, complete anarchy, going on behind her and she keeps singing calmly even when she is turned upside down. One of the lyrics in the song is "nothing's gonna change my world". Every time I had an urge to binge I would just imagine the video and hear those lyrics and let the feelings pass through me. I accepted them and they did not have to

"change my world" or make me react to them. It made them much easier to deal with. I have not seen that video since the 90's. It's interesting the things your brain can come up with. Whatever works, go with it."

Clare

Dismiss the binge urge

A great way to distance yourself from a binge craving is to dismiss it. The only power a binge urge sensation has over you is the power and meaning you give to them. So give it no significance or meaning. Normalize it. Ignore it. Dismiss it. Brush it off. Detach yourself from the sensation. Be indifferent to it. Think of it as just another occurrence, like a sneeze or a shiver. Something that happens, then passes, that requires no further attention. Just think: "Oh well, here's another binge urge, it's just a sensation, it'll pass in time."

The more **dismissive** you are towards your binge urges the less power they have over you. It's like the school bully trying to taunt you into a fight. Just let the bully be there, taunting you, but don't give the bully the time of day. Just ignore the bully and walk away. Think, **"WHATEVER!"**.

Let go of any fear towards a binge urge

If we let go of any fear we feel towards a binge urge, it makes them easier to dismiss.

If someone unexpectedly jumped out at you and said, "Boo!" you'd probably get a fright, the fight-or-flight response would kick in, but it would only last for a few moments as you would quickly calm down when you realize there is no reason to be afraid. However, for most people, when a binge urge strikes, they react as though they really are being attacked. They stay in the stressed fight-or-flight state, usually until they end up bingeing on food.

We don't get anxious about a pounding heart just after we've been running because we know the exercise was the cause of the palpitations. Nor do we get anxious after having stubbed a toe. If we know what causes something it doesn't incite so much fear. At the end of the day, a binge urge is just a bodily sensation. It's simply fight-or-flight chemicals rushing through your body. **It's just biology**. You are not going to come to any harm. **There is nothing to fear**. These feelings and sensations cannot harm or hurt you. It is okay to experience a binge urge.

A simple technique you can use to reduce any fear associated with binge urge sensations is to mentally personify a binge urge as something silly, like a cartoon character.

Perhaps, imagine a binge urge as Daffy Duck quacking in your ear, trying to taunt you to binge. You can just think to yourself, "Silly Daffy!" and move on with your day.

It sounds silly, but these subtle mind tricks can give you that extra edge to defeat a binge urge. Play around and see what works best for you. **Try to have some fun with this**.

MUSCLE RELEASE TECHNIQUE

Sometimes the pull towards a binge can be very strong. Sometimes we barely have a moment to breathe never mind cultivate a space between the craving and our response. In those moments when the urge feels overwhelming and you need a quick fix, I want you to use the Binge Code Muscle Release Technique.

Muscle Release Technique

1. Take a very deep breath in and hold it.

2. Tense every muscle in your body for 5 seconds (this means you are contracting your toes, thighs, calves, buttocks, stomach, chest, arms and hands. You can even clench your jaw if you want. The more muscles you squeeze tight, the better).

3. Release every muscle as you slowly exhale.

4. Rest for 10 seconds and then repeat 3-5 times. This should take you roughly less than 2 minutes.

(If you are somewhere more public, you can just clench your hands into fists for 5-10 seconds).

Try it now and notice the effects yourself. You should feel an instant wave of relaxation using this technique.

This is an extremely powerful technique for calming your nervous system. By constricting your muscles, you trick your brain into thinking that you're running away from a threat, so it turns off the fight or flight response. This helps to create a space, a moment of calm and makes rational thought possible again.

Practice it a few times and have it ready to go. Whenever you feel like the binge urge is going to overwhelm you, apply the technique. Don't debate it, don't question it, just do it.

THE CALM BREATH TECHNIQUE

If you wish to calm yourself further you can use the Calm Breath Technique.

The Calm Breath

1. Inhale through your nose to the count of 4, breathe deeply into your belly and chest area and feel it expand.

2. Exhale through your nose, slowly count to 4 (or whatever rhythm is comfortable), allowing your body to relax and release tension.

3. Repeat for 2-5 minutes.

Please don't underestimate how effective this simple tool can be. One of the most basic, most effective tools soldiers have to keep their cool while under fire is controlling their breathing. Yoga masters have known about the power of the breath for thousands of years. Scientific research is showing that deep breathing is one of the most effective ways to lower everyday stress levels and improve a variety of health factors ranging from mood to metabolism.

The key to the Calm Breath is that you slowly inhale into both your chest and relaxed belly (don't suck your stomach in). You should feel your ribcage and abdomen expand as you fill the entirety of your lungs with oxygen with each breath. If you feel comfortable you can increase the count to 5, the deeper the breath the stronger the sense of relaxation.

"The beauty of deep breathing is that I can do it anytime, anywhere. It doesn't matter if I'm at home or at work, if I'm indoors or out, if I'm by myself or in a crowd. Whenever I feel that twinge of agitation, the one that tells me all I need is a candy bar or two. I put myself into Zen10 mode. I stop and focus on those deep breaths for three minutes. Inhale, exhale. Inhale, exhale. Much better."

- R Tara

"But my binge urge isn't going away!"

At this point we are not getting rid of the binge urge. This is about creating a space between the discomfort of the urge and your reaction to that discomfort. By learning to be more comfortable with any feelings of discomfort you are more able to ignore and dismiss the urge.

"But I REALLY want to binge on food!"

Let's think about this. When you say, "I really want to binge on food!" what you are really saying is "I really want to remove the **discomfort** of experiencing a binge craving". You don't really want to binge, you want to get rid of the **uncomfortable feelings**. Again, by learning to be more comfortable with feeling uncomfortable, the binge urge won't bother you so much.

"But I can't stand being uncomfortable!"

Binge urges can be uncomfortable, but they are not unbearable. I am sure you can imagine many other things a lot more uncomfortable than a binge urge. Giving birth, breaking your leg, scalding yourself, the list goes on.

"But I really, really want to binge on food!"

No, you don't. You don't want to binge. You don't want what it does to your life. You don't want how it makes you feel afterwards. You don't want to spend the rest of your life trapped in the misery of binge eating. Why else would you be reading this book?

"But I'll go crazy if I don't give in!"

You haven't gone crazy yet, so don't worry you won't. By not giving into your cravings you will see that your world will not fall apart.

"But I am feeling too anxious!!!"

Anxiety and binge urges go hand in hand. Sometimes in the midst of a binge urge, we can feel restless and twitchy, as though our body is exploding with nervous energy. If you feel yourself vibrating or buzzing like this, then I would suggest applying a few more rounds of the Muscle Release Technique. Or alternatively you can just move your body. Go for a brisk walk, run on the spot, just start shaking your limbs out. Moving is a great way to release tension and stress.

"But I feel deprived if I don't binge!"

You will only feel deprived if you think that you're missing out on something. You are not missing out. You are not depriving yourself. Binge eating is a false friend. It gives you nothing. You're not broken and you do not need to binge on food to be fixed.

If anything, it's the opposite; by constantly bingeing on food you are depriving yourself from living free from the stress, self-loathing and anxiety of constantly bingeing.

"My urges are getting stronger!"

Binge cravings have a strong tendency to ebb and flow like the tide. Sometimes they are stronger, sometimes they are weaker. This is just the nature of the binge urge. And yes, sometimes that can be very frustrating, but just allow the binge urge some space to do as it pleases. Know that in time it will decrease and fade away. Like a wave, its passing is inevitable.

"But I want to fight the binge urge to get rid of it!"

Certainly, it makes sense that our initial instinct is to fight the binge urge. It's a perceived danger so we want to wrestle it to the ground and throttle it out of existence. But in all honesty, how many times in the past has that been effective for you?

I'm not asking you to like the binge urge. I'm sure you'd rather the feeling wasn't there. That's understandable. But you don't have to struggle and fight it, that would just be adding suffering to suffering. The bottom line is that the feeling of a binge urge is less than ideal, but it is not intolerable. Remind yourself that the binge urge is just a feeling, it is not dangerous and does not need to be fought. Allow the urge to rise and fall again. Tap into your zen mind and let the discomfort pass through you like the wind blowing through the leaves of a tree.

I know how challenging this can be. At times not giving into your binge urges can feel exhausting and difficult and stressful. It may not feel like freedom. It may feel like the exact opposite of freedom. In those moments stay mindful until there is enough time and space between you and the binge urge. Only then can you feel the freedom.

GET ON WITH YOUR DAY

After applying the Zen10 technique, I want you to engage yourself in an activity. Psychologists know that concentrating on two things at the same time is very hard. If you are focused on an activity it takes your mind off the binge urge.

I would suggest something that involves physical movement and something that takes you away from any possible binge foods, preferably to a safe environment. Something as simple as going for a walk can be extremely effective.

Here are some other suggestions:

- Listen to a Binge Code Meditation audio.
- Take a bath.
- Talk to a friend.
- Work or play on your computer.
- Immerse yourself in a project or hobby.
- Listen to your favorite music.
- Watch some interesting videos on YouTube.com.
- Work in the garden.
- If you have children, play some games with them.
- Clean out or organize that cupboard/desk/drawer/space.

AFTER 10 MINUTES

If you manage to delay bingeing on food for 10 minutes, congratulate yourself. Well done!

What should you do next?

Take a moment to tune in and see how you feel. If the binge urge has passed, great! Move on with your day. If the binge urge is still present, first of all, **don't panic**. Sometimes a binge urge can take a bit longer to pass. You now have a few options for your next course of action:

Delay Further

If you feel strong enough you can try to delay the binge urge for a further 10 minutes.

COACH CORNER

I think I delayed acting on binge urges for what felt like months at a time, okay maybe I'm exaggerating a little here, but that was what it felt like at the time. I'd always do it **little by little.** I'd let my mind race thinking about bingeing. I'd tell myself I could binge, but then I'd challenge myself to get through the next meal first. "Eat this now and binge later if you still want to." I'd be telling myself. This can be another great way to delay, just in small segments, pushing yourself further and further each time.

Catherine Liberty

Assess if you are in fact, just hungry

If, after 10 minutes you still have strong cravings to binge on food then you may need to assess whether or not you are actually just hungry. Binge cravings tend to be more fleeting whereas **real hunger tends to be more stable and less fluctuating**. As you progress through The Binge Code you will begin to develop a much clearer understanding of what real hunger feels like and you'll be able to clearly differentiate between the two.

What if I want to binge after 10 minutes?

The truth is that you're learning to put yourself in the driver's seat. You're opening up space to make choices where there was none before. You're learning to feel the power of this for yourself. The choices of your old habits have not been taken away from you. You can go back to those choices, if that's the decision you want to make. What I would say though is this: you already know what the old choices do to you. You've repeatedly seen their negative effects on your life. How would your life be changed by making new choices at this time? You'll never know unless you try. Wouldn't it be powerful to see and explore this? Even if it is just for the next 10 minutes… Give yourself the freedom to see how you feel about a new way of responding. It could be the most life-changing present you'll ever give yourself. I know it was for me.

Getting a sense of Zen10

It can be helpful to practice the Zen10 technique before you actually have any binge cravings. For example, you could practice during your morning shower. Turn the hot water cold for 10 seconds or so and apply the Zen10 technique to any uncomfortable sensations. Feel the cold, but delay acting on the cold sensations. Realise that your body can easily handle the cold, it is your reactive mind you have to convince.

Zen 10 Technique Summary

I know that we covered a range of ideas and concepts here, but try not to overcomplicate this. Really, your primary focus is to cultivate a sense of space between a craving and the need to act on that craving. And then just rest your mind there. Eventually, with practice, whenever you say the phrase "Zen10" you will feel yourself automatically snap into that protective mindset.

The Zen10 Technique Summary

1. When you notice you are craving a binge urge say the phrase "Zen10" to yourself.

2. Cultivate a sense of space between the craving and your need to act on that craving. Rest your mind in that space.

3. Wait 10 minutes before taking any action towards a binge. When the time is up, see if you can extend it by another 10 minutes. Try to keep going until the urge subsides.

To help cultivate a space you can:

- Use mental visualization to strengthen your resolve.

- Dismiss any binge urges. Brush them off and let them be.

- Apply the Muscle Release Technique for powerful urges.

- Apply the Calm Breath for deeper relaxation.

- Move on with your day and focus your attention elsewhere.

Following these steps won't magically get rid of binge urges (I wish it could) but it will ease the intensity of those binge urges and it's a great tool to use whilst you progress through the rest of the Binge Code Program.

Download the "Bust binge cravings" guided meditation audio from www.thebingecode.com/bonus

PART 2

BREAK FREE FROM THE BINGE TRAPS

AND FULLY REMOVE ANY BINGE URGES FROM YOUR LIFE ONCE AND FOR ALL

The Zen10 technique is a great tool to help you overcome any binge urges, but it's not enough. In truth, it's just a **temporary band-aid**. It doesn't resolve the real underlying problem; the binge traps. If you are stuck in any of the binge traps you will always be prone to binge urges. To fully remove any binge urges from your life you must undo the binge traps.

Here is a quick recap of the seven binge traps.

THE 7 BINGE TRAPS

Trap 1: The Diet Trap

Trap 2: The Yo-Yo Blood Sugar Trap

Trap 3: The Nutritional Deficiency Trap

Trap 4: The Habit Trap

Trap 5: The Food Rules Trap

Trap 6: The False Friend Trap

Trap 7: The Inner Critic Trap

To begin with we are going to focus on the first three traps: The Diet Trap, The Yo-Yo Blood Sugar Trap and The Nutritional Deficiency Trap. These traps are all based around your physical body.

This is a great place to start. By breaking free from these traps you set yourself up with a really strong, **solid foundation** for the rest of the program.

We are going to explore each trap in detail and then I am going to provide you with the key to unlock each trap. By following this stage, you can expect to experience a dramatic reduction in your binge urges and food obsession. You can start right now, apply these steps to your life and notice a big impact in just **a few days**.

Let's get started with the first trap then: The Diet Trap.

THE DIET TRAP

For a lot of you, this is going to be a huge player in your binge urges. It certainly was for me.

It's true that as a society we are diet obsessed. We live in a diet culture. We are constantly sold the idea that being thin will make us more attractive, more successful and more happy. According to some surveys up to 50% of women are on a diet at any given time. One in two women are dieting right this moment!

So this brings me to the question, with so many people dieting, why aren't we all thin by now? Really, where are the successful dieters? I've yet to meet one. And come to think of it, why are we in the middle of an obesity epidemic? It's clear that something isn't adding up.

Perhaps unsurprisingly then, research shows us diets do the opposite of their intended purpose. Not only do **diets not work**, in the long run they **make us gain weight**.

Research shows us that within four years, 95% of dieters will gain back all the weight they have lost and two out of five dieters **end up heavier** than they were before they lost weight.

The most reliable evidence that dieting leads to weight gain comes from a study of 1,600 identical twins. Those who dieted, weighed more at the beginning of the study, showed more weight variability and had gained more weight four years later.

It is a scientific fact: **dieting causes people to overeat**. All dieting is yo-yo dieting in practice. Whilst successful dieters seem to be non-existent, people who repeatedly gain and lose weight are abundant. Over time these weight fluctuations gradually lead to a heavier weight overall. As a nation we would be thinner if no-one ever dieted. Many of my clients are overweight because of yo-yo dieting.

Perhaps most importantly for you is the fact that dieting also **leads to binge eating**. One of the most famous and respected studies ever conducted on the effects of food restriction in humans was the 1944 Ancel Keys Semi-Starvation Study. The participants were put on diets of 1,600 calories per day for 6 months. Over time they began to suffer from side effects such as anxiety, food obsession, depression and binge eating. Once the experiment ended, some of the men ate more than five thousand calories a day and continued to eat even when their stomachs were stuffed (sound familiar anyone?)

Here are a few more interesting facts about food restriction and binge eating:

- In one large study girls who dieted frequently were twelve times more likely to report binge eating.
- Boys who dieted frequently were seven times more likely to binge eat.
- When food is restricted through the day, binge urges become more frequent.

The stricter the diet and food restriction is, the stronger the binge urges are in response. It is as though every diet has an equal and opposite binge to counter it.

These rules apply to everyone. If the healthiest, happiest person on the planet restricted their food intake, they would make themselves susceptible to powerful binge urges.

Let's explore the relationship between restriction and binge eating further. I've broken this down into simple stages to help you grasp how food restriction can lead to bingeing.

How food restriction can lead to binge eating

You restrict your food intake

There are many reasons why people may restrict their food intake. These reasons include:

- Avoiding major food groups like carbohydrates or fats based on the misguided assumption that it's healthy to do so.
- Avoiding specific foods, or on rare occasions, entire food groups, due to food allergies and intolerances.
- Embarking on restrictive detox programs in the belief that they will be beneficial to overall health.
- A direct attempt to lose some weight by going on a calorie restrictive diet and/or over-exercising (by far the most popular reason).

You ignore your hunger pangs

When you are actively restricting your food intake you may start to ignore your hunger pangs. As your body fights back with hunger, you fight back with denial and so the war against yourself begins.

Your biology begins to fight back

There are three essentials that we need in life to survive, these are:

1. Air
2. Water
3. Food

If we do not get enough air, water or food then we will die. To prevent us from dying, the human body naturally evolved powerful survival mechanisms over millions of years to ensure that we breathe, drink and eat.

As you continue to restrict your food intake and ignore your hunger, your body reacts by adjusting your hormones and neurotransmitters (the chemical messengers that tell your body what do). Your levels of leptin decrease. This decrease triggers your appetite and leads directly to powerful food thoughts, cravings and unavoidable urges to binge eat.

You start to experience a new type of powerful, uncontrollable hunger. You no longer feel mild hunger pangs, instead your hunger comes in sudden, erratic bursts. You feel panicked and scared by these intense episodes of hunger and you start to realize that it's becoming increasingly difficult to stay in control around food.

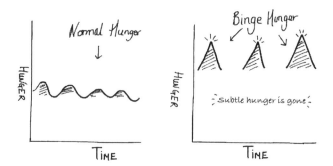

You hit the weight loss plateau

In the beginning, most diets do lead to some weight loss (although a considerable amount of this is a result of water loss rather than fat reduction). However, after a certain point, most people hit a weight loss plateau.

At a plateau, your weight stubbornly stays the same even though you're continuing to eat less food. Why?

Your body responds by slowing down its internal workings (basal metabolic rate, or BMR) so you expend less energy and can survive on fewer calories. Your BMR accounts for about **two-thirds** of your body's total energy needs, so any change to your BMR at all can have a huge impact on your ability to lose weight. In this state your body is programed to store any food you do eat as fat, rather than allowing you to expend it as energy.

You lose your get up and go, your drive, your vitality. You feel sluggish and foggy with low energy.

You feel driven to binge on food

Every cell in your body is now screaming out for you to **EAT!** You're unable to fight back any longer. You don't understand why food thoughts and cravings are taking over your life and you can no longer resist the urge to eat, no matter how hard you try.

Suddenly you find yourself bingeing on food. At this point it may feel like someone else has taken over your entire body.

You lose the ability to feel satisfied and this can be really scary. Where normally you would feel too full, now it seems like you are able to eat and eat and eat and never feel satisfied.

You panic and try to compensate for the food eaten

After losing control and bingeing, intense feelings of fear, panic, disgust, failure and guilt overwhelm you. You swear to yourself that you're going to compensate for this binge by not eating for rest of the day, or by only having salad for the rest of the week, or by getting straight back on that diet tomorrow.

You get stuck in the Diet Trap

Each binge leads to greater desire to restrict and diet, which leads to more binge urges. And so you go, round and round, in cycles of bingeing and dieting, **stuck in the Diet Trap.**

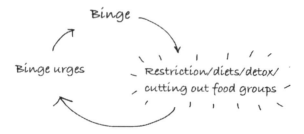

Restriction Trap

So, there you have it, how a simple diet can lead to a life trapped in a cycle of binge eating and restriction. This is not a sign of weakness or a lack of willpower. This is your body fighting back. This is your body working to naturally defend itself. This is your body willing you to survive.

Think about your history around food. Do you have a history of yo-yo diets and food restriction? If so, then you know The Diet Trap plays a big role in your binge urges.

DIET TRAP BINGE EXAMPLES

The "I am so hungry I could eat a horse" binge

When you experience a ravishing, overwhelming, powerful binge urge, where you just want to uncontrollably eat everything in sight.

The evening/ night time binge

You've been under-eating/ restricting/ or 'being good' all day. Now it's the evening time. You're no longer running a million miles per minute. Your kids are sleeping, the emails have slowed down, you're no longer at work… it's just you, your hunger and the contents of the fridge.

HOW TO BREAK FREE FROM THE DIET TRAP

The first thing we need to do is to retrain our minds and bodies to expect food often and regularly. To do this we need to **feed ourselves regularly**. This involves eating 3 meals and 3 snacks each day with no more than a 3 hour break in-between each meal.

It can help to set your times prior to starting. An example of this would be:

8.00am: Breakfast time
10.30am: Morning snack
1.00pm: Lunch time
3.30pm: Afternoon snack
6.00pm: Dinner time
8.30pm: Evening snack

Alternatively you could have 6 small meals of equal size. Whatever works best for you.

By doing this you are telling your body, "You don't have to force me to binge on large amounts of food now because I will provide you with more food soon."

It will take time for your body to trust that it can have more food later, but if you continue to eat something regularly it will become biologically reconditioned to know that it will always have access to food. You start to set a **rhythm for your body**. It will know when to expect food. It will know when it should start to feel hungry.

This works great if you are a binge-grazer. This is where you find yourself continually snacking on food all day long without a clear break between meals. Studies show that continual snacking interferes with hunger and satiety hormones. The body likes the break in-between to work on digestion and stabilizing blood sugar levels. Try to be mindful of continually grazing on food and instead wait to eat at your allocated times.

So many people are tempted to skip lunch or breakfast but this is absolutely not an option. To do so would leave you feeling vulnerable to binge urges. If you are too hungry at your next meal you are likely to gravitate towards less nutritious foods, you'll want to eat more rapidly and you'll be able to eat for longer before feeling satisfied. Even if you're consuming thousands of calories during evening binges, it's the initial restriction throughout the day that may be driving those binge urges. Also, studies show that people who skip meals during the day and then eat lots in the evening, tend to be more overweight than those who eat regularly throughout the day.

Eating regularly also helps to stabilize your blood sugar levels which will automatically suppress your appetite.

"What if I'm not hungry?"

You can wait a little longer, but I would say 4 hours needs to be the absolute longest you ever leave between meals, even when you are not noticing a lot of hunger.

Even if you do not feel hungry, when it is time to eat, you should try and eat something. Even something small. Binge eating has made your internal food regulatory system unreliable. Eating in a mechanical way like this is important until you can trust your own hunger and satiety cues.

"Do I have to eat breakfast?"

Yes. Eating a meal in the morning within an hour of waking is recommended by the British Dietetic Association. A Harvard University study indicated that people who miss breakfast are four times more likely than others to become obese. Further research shows people who skip breakfast also tend to have higher cholesterol, elevated insulin levels and larger waist circumferences. That's a lot of good reasons to eat breakfast!

———

EAT ENOUGH FOOD

Along with eating regularly we also want to ensure that we eat enough food. Binges can occur from even gradual, minor under-eating over a period of a few days. So how much food does the average person need to get them through the day?

In 1993 the US Food and Drug Administration (FDA) was originally going to state that the daily number of recommended calories was 2,350. However, the FDA then decided that this number was too cumbersome. So to make things simpler, 2000 calories was used instead. That's 350 calories (or approximately one whole meal/snack) less than the actual daily recommendations!

Today, based on current research, it seems that even the original number was an underestimation. A highly valid method of measuring energy expenditure called the "doubly labeled water" method provides further insight into this. Findings from experiments where this method of research was used revealed that women and men (who are moderately active and maintaining normal weights) expend around 2400 and 3050 calories per day respectively. That is, **400-1050 calories** more than the FDA's food label recommendations!

What this boils down to is that it is going to be impossible to stop binge eating on 1500 calories a day if your body's requirement is over 2000. **Yes, impossible**.

This information will be especially beneficial for you if you live in fear of weight gain. It will hopefully give you a better understanding what your body needs in terms of nourishment and fuel.

Personally I don't go under **2200 calories a day**, this suits my needs. I'm 5'2 female and relatively active. However, it's important to understand that everyone is different and not one size fits all. You may need to adjust up or down. A rule of thumb, if you are still experiencing intense binge urges after a few weeks then try and up the amount you eat and see if you notice a reduction in your urges. This is usually a sign that your body is needing more nutrition. Please consult with a registered dietitian before changing your diet or calorific intake.

In our coaching program we worked with a woman who was a semi-professional athlete. We tried several approaches and still couldn't understand why her binge urges were so powerful. That was until one day when she realized that because of how active she was in her training and at work, she needed to be consuming around 3800 calories per day! Pretty extreme case I know, but it's definitely worth considering whether you're eating enough food throughout the day.

A handy trick to ensure you are eating enough calories is to eat nutrient dense foods for snacks. Perhaps a combination of things like nuts, seeds and nut butters. They won't make you feel overly full but offer an easy way to meet your calorie and nutrient needs.

"I've just binged what should I do now?"

You may be tempted to avoid eating completely for the rest of the day to avoid weight gain, but, as we know, food restriction only leads straight back onto the Diet Trap roller coaster. This is completely counterproductive. The best approach is to continue to eat something every 3 hours or less as this will help to get your body back into the cycle of regular food. At the same time feel free to reduce the calorie content of your next meal to compensate for the binge. I suggest eating a small snack or a balanced smoothie. Then after this, resume your regular eating plan when the next meal time comes around. Even if you are over your calorie limit, ensure that you still eat something.

"But I eat more than that each day!"

Not everyone who binges on food restricts their food intake. If you are eating a lot more than this each day, please don't fret. I would suggest focusing on **spreading your nutrition throughout your day**.

Ensure you are getting an ample breakfast and lunch so that you're not famished by dinner time. In doing so you will rapidly feel more in control around food and less likely to binge. In time, as you progress through the program, as your body begins to rebalance, you will discover the ideal amount of food that works best for you.

DIET TRAP SUMMARY

Under-eating leads to over-eating. Let go of restrictive diets, they don't work. Eat enough food to satisfy your biological requirements. Spread your nutrition throughout the day by avoiding gaps of longer than 3 hours without eating. Try not to graze in-between meals. This will help set a rhythm for your body.

2: THE YO-YO BLOOD SUGAR TRAP

I worked out quickly, in the earliest days of my binge eating, that having heaps of sweets, lollies, chips and sugary foods around the house was just not a good idea. So, I made sure that I didn't have those 'binge foods' in my pantry in the hope of avoiding bingeing. It wasn't a terrible plan. But the truth was, that when I did have the urge to binge, the foods I'd banned from my house were the only ones I wanted. So, I'd silently praise the 24/7 shopping world we live in and I'd go and buy all the crisps, candy, donuts, pies and fried foods I wanted. Then I'd return home and secretly binge on them (if I hadn't already eaten them all in the car).

Chances are when you binge on food, you don't binge on salads. You binge on muffins, pies, sweets, fizzy drinks and donuts. Mostly refined carbohydrates. The problem with refined carbohydrates is that your body finds them very appealing sources of energy. They are easily broken down into simple sugars and are quickly absorbed into the blood stream causing a rise in blood sugar levels. This causes an immediate reaction in your body because high levels of sugar are toxic to the cells. So, your body releases a surge of insulin which pulls the sugar from the blood. Unfortunately, insulin is too good at its job and instead of reducing blood sugar levels to normal, it sends them plummeting lower than it was originally, to sub-normal levels.

As your brain is entirely fueled by glucose, low blood sugar levels can lead to many issues including rapid mood swings, reduced reaction times and depression. In this state we feel groggy, tired and unmotivated. Also, the more insulin you have in your blood, the more likely you are to store any excess calories as fat.

But most importantly for us, low blood sugar levels makes us **crave fatty, sugary foods.** A study published in the International Journal of Eating Disorders found that when blood sugar levels were too low, the desire to binge on carbohydrate (sugar) rich foods would intensify (Volume 9, 1990). It's your body's way of trying to get back in balance, of trying to restore it's blood sugar levels back to normal. It is an **uncontrollable instinct** that kicks in when your blood sugar drops.

These cravings can lead to another binge on refined carbohydrates, which leads to another blood sugar crash, which leads to another binge, which leads to another crash and so the cycle continues, going from one sugar spike to the next. Sugar leads to more sugar, to more sugar to more and more and you become trapped in the **Yo-Yo Blood Sugar Trap**.

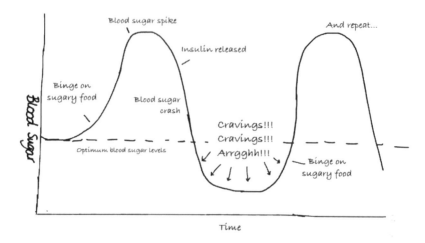

Even if you have never dieted or restricted your food in the past you can still get stuck in the Yo-Yo Blood Sugar Trap. Do you find your energy levels fluctuate throughout the day? Are you usually sleepy an hour or so after eating? Do you have regular cravings for something sweet? Are you bingeing on chocolate, crisps, sugary drinks or rice cakes? If so you may be stuck in the Yo-Yo Blood Sugar Trap.

YO-YO BLOOD SUGAR BINGE EXAMPLES

The sugar binge

Where you have cravings for all things sugary and sweet (including refined carbohydrates like pasta and white bread).

The hangover binge

After a night of indulging in alcohol your blood sugar levels plummet and you crave sugary fatty foods.

HOW TO BREAK FREE FROM THE YO-YO BLOOD SUGAR TRAP

At this point I do want to stress that the information provided here is from trusted, qualified nutritionists but is meant as guidance only. Please see a registered dietitian before undertaking any meal plans. With that said, let's get into this!

The solution to the Yo-Yo Blood Sugar Trap is to start eating **balanced** food. In one study, 20 bulimic women were put on a sugar stabilizing diet to see if it would help with their urges to binge and purge. Within three weeks all of the 20 had completely stopped bingeing and all of them remained free from binges in the long term too (Dalvit-McPhillips, 1984). That's a pretty amazing result when the only thing they did was steady yo-yo-ing blood sugar.

Firstly, we need to ensure each meal (and preferably each snack) has a combination of all 3 primary macronutrients. That means a serving of **complex carbohydrates, protein and fat** in each meal.

Doing this will help to:

- Slow down the absorption of glucose into the bloodstream and prevent sugar highs/crashes.
- Slow digestion so you feel fuller for longer and absorb more nutrition from your food.
- Make you feel more satisfied after each meal.

So what's the best ratio of carbohydrates, proteins and fats?

I suggest you start with meals that are roughly **50% carbohydrates, 25% proteins and 25% fats** (by calories, not volume). This can be thought of simply as a 2/1/1 ratio.

Roughly half of your plate dedicated to carbs, a quarter dedicated to proteins and a quarter dedicated to fats. This isn't an exact science. Just a rough ballpark. You don't need to portion out your plate exactly. This does not need to be "perfect". Over time as you settle into the program you can adjust these percentages to suit your individual needs. For example, you may find that a larger percentage of protein and fat with each meal helps you feel more balanced, satisfied and craving free. This personal knowledge and insight will come in time, but for now just stick with the **2/1/1 ratio**.

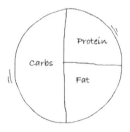

Some examples of this would be:

1. Half a plate of rice and broccoli, one quarter chicken and one quarter Avocado
2. Half a plate of whole-grain pasta, one quarter fish and one quarter cream-based sauce
3. Half a plate of baked potato & vegetables, one half roasted meat with gravy
4. Half a plate of fresh salad and half a plate of cheese omelette

Ok, so let's discuss the role of carbohydrates

When we are talking about carbs we don't mean the refined, over-processed, sugary carbs like muffins, juices, fizzy drinks, donuts, or added ingredients like high-fructose corn syrup (which is believed to be the culprit behind many health concerns such as obesity and mental health issues).

The carbohydrates we are referring to are the real, whole, nourishing, plant-based foods that humans have survived on for thousands of years.

There's been a rise in "carbophobia" (a fear of carbs) and many health experts believe that this alone is causing more and more incidences of binge eating. Carbs are not the bad guys, they provide us with an abundance of minerals that our bodies need to function normally.

Carbs play a vital role in our brain health and help manufacture the production of serotonin. Serotonin is the main neurotransmitter regulating our mood and appetite, so it's an important one! When we restrict the intake of carbohydrates put ourselves at risk of lower serotonin levels, which in turn can affect our mood (Wurtman RJ, Brain serotonin, carbohydrate-craving, obesity and depression, 1995).

Fiber and starch are the two types of complex carbohydrates. Fiber is especially important because it not only helps stabilize blood sugar levels, it also helps us to feel full and satiated after eating and helps to promote bowel regularity.

Types of complex carbs include:

- All fruits and vegetables
- Nuts
- Beans and lentils
- Whole grains
- Whole wheat bread
- Cereals
- Quinoa
- Rice

The importance of protein

Protein has incredible power over our appetites. "Protein makes you feel fuller for longer by balancing your blood sugar; it modulates your appetite and greatly reduces binge cravings." (Rolls et al, 1988). Studies show that the most effective way to stimulate the release of the satiety hormones which tell the brain that you're full, is to eat protein-rich foods.

Protein is a component of every cell in your body. Your body uses it to build and repair tissue, bones, muscles, cartilage, skin and blood and you also need it to make enzymes, hormones and other body chemicals.

Ideas for adding protein to your meal plan:

- Protein can be found in many different types of foods, even vegetables, but the highest sources are those that come from animals like meat, dairy, eggs and fish.
- Eat more legumes (beans) as they have about 7g of protein per serving whereas other whole grains like brown rice and whole wheat bread have 4-5g of protein per serving.
- Eat eggs (including the yolk) - many people stick to eating only egg whites but the egg yolk contains carotenoids, lutein and vitamin E which can all provide excellent health benefits and disease protection.
- Understand that protein doesn't just have to come from meat - legumes, tofu products and seafood can be great sources of protein.

"Protein sources that have been great for me: protein powder in fruit smoothies, hard boiled eggs, cottage cheese, high quality yogurt with lots of probiotics. Tofu squares are good. They're firm so they can travel with you and they come in a variety of flavors. Pre-made protein shakes are kind of icky tasting but have been really great for me on days where I feel in danger of bingeing."

Tania B

Let's discuss fat

Fat. For many of you even the word alone can strike a shiver of anxiety in your heart. The truth is, for years we have been getting fat all wrong.

We are now being informed that the "low-fat campaign" which kicked off in the 90s was in fact a mistake. It was based on little scientific evidence and may have caused unintended bad health consequences. A *Journal of the American Medical Association* study recently revealed that a "low fat" diet showed the greatest drop in energy expenditure and increased insulin resistance (which is a precursor to diabetes) compared with a low carbohydrate and low glycaemic index (GI) diet. They are basically saying that low fat diets are crippling metabolic rates, causing obesity and even increasing diabetes.

In the United States, obesity has rocketed despite the percentage of calorie consumption from fat falling from 40 per cent to 30 per cent in the past 30 years. One reason is that the food industry compensated by replacing saturated fat with added sugar. Many of the top experts are now trying to undo this damage and spread the word about the importance of dietary fat. Sweden recently became the first Western nation to adopt a high-fat approach to nutrition.

This belief that 'fat makes you fat' is based on a myth. Eating fat helps to curb overeating and it allows you to feel full, content and satisfied after eating.

So, what are the right fats, exactly? According to Dr Hyman, they include coconut oil, extra-virgin olive oil, coconut milk, avocado, fatty fish like sardines and wild salmon, nuts and seeds, olives. Also, include fats from grazing animals like butter, egg yolks and ghee (clarified butter).

We don't want to get obsessed with "healthy" and "unhealthy" fats so, rather than thinking about fats that you should limit, try instead to focus on all of those wonderful healthful fats you can add to your meals.

Here are a few suggestions you can start putting into your diet today:

- Almonds
- Avocados
- Egg yolks
- Fish
- Walnuts

- Cheese
- Extra virgin olive oil
- Nut Butters

If you have been avoiding fat, take your time reintroducing it into your diet. Start with small portions and build it up. It may take a while for your digestive system to relearn how to process fat.

COACH CORNER

I'd remind myself that after eating food containing fat I'd experience less binge urges, feel fuller for longer and even absorb all of the other wonderful nutrients from vegetables. I'd visualise my body becoming healthier as I allowed myself to eat in this way. It's so important to challenge that old mindset.

Catherine Liberty

Fruits and veggies

I know that eating lots of fruits and veggies can make you feel great and they can be so nourishing, but if you are lacking any macronutrients, you'll experience binge urges and lower energy. So make sure you tweak your meals to ensure they are adequately balanced, for example, adding some avocado or nuts for fats, or some fish or tofu for protein.

"Earlier in the week I had a real craving for fresh fruits. Once I'd eaten the fruit salad I continued to feel good and energized for about an hour and a half, but then had a little dip. It was almost like there was gap in my digestive system or something and it felt sort of 'uneven'.

I thought about how to add some fats and protein and decided, the next time I had the fruit salad to add some organic nuts and seeds - and this worked brilliantly to extend my satiety and make my mood and body feel energized for longer."

Tara

Stabilizing blood sugar further

Here are a few extra steps you can follow to help stabilize your blood sugar.

- Alcohol is a nightmare for our blood sugar as our body processes alcohol as sugar. If we overindulge, the next day our sugar cravings sky rocket which can lead to huge cravings. Avoid drinking for at least the first few months of the program. If you need to have a drink, have one to two units a day at most (a small glass of wine or shot of spirits is 1.5 units).
- Some foods are better at stabilizing blood sugar than others. Try include more quinoa, bulgur (cracked wheat), whole rye, whole-grain barley, wild rice and buckwheat in your meal plan.
- Likewise try including more legumes, such as lentils and kidney beans and see if you notice a difference.
- Instead of eating sugar filled cereal in the morning try some porridge oats or eggs (boiled, poached, scrambled or as an omelette) for breakfast. A solid, blood sugar stabilizing breakfast can really help set you up for the day.

If you are vegan or vegetarian

Being vegan or vegetarian is totally acceptable within The Binge Code program. However, just be careful you don't load up on carbohydrates at the expense of the other food groups. Just make sure you are balancing your meals with enough proteins (quinoa, chickpeas, beans) and fats (oils, avocados).

Zen10 your sugar cravings

The Zen10 technique is a great tool to help combat any sugar cravings. Just recently, I noticed that my love for dark chocolate was triggering my sweet tooth to the point where it was making me feel a little off-balance. The more I ate, the more I craved it. So I decided to apply the Zen10 technique towards my chocolate cravings. It work wonderfully. By the time 10 minutes had passed I was usually so busy doing something else, that any chocolate cravings just slipped from my mind. After about a week, my cravings vanished. I still have dark chocolate from time to time, but I am not craving it like before. I recommend you keep the Zen10 technique in your back pocket, ready to use to combat any cravings you may have.

YO-YO BLOOD SUGAR TRAP SUMMARY

Aim to have each meal (and preferably each snack) consist of a ratio of roughly 50% complex carbohydrates, 25% proteins and 25% fats. This will do wonders to stabilize your blood sugar levels and reduce your sugar carvings. Over time, discover the ratio that works best for you, so you feel fuller for longer and more satisfied after each meal.

3: THE NUTRITIONAL DEFICIENCY TRAP

I tried to eat healthy, I really did. But for me personally, healthy meant eating as little fat in my meals as possible. In my mind fat = bad. Rice cakes, salads, apples, zero fat yogurt and Diet Coke were all common staples in my diet. Is it little wonder that I began to experience massive cravings to consume (you guessed it)... fat.

This leads me to the next Binge Trap, I call this one the **Nutritional Deficiency Trap**. Even though you may be feeding your body lots of calories, you may be nutritionally deficient, if you are:

- Eating the same, familiar (safe) foods over and over.
- Eating food lacking adequate nutrition, (fast food or overly processed foods).
- Cutting out whole macronutrient food groups (such as carbohydrates) from your diet.
- Over stressed, overworked and just overdoing it in general.

(At the time when I was binge eating all four of these applied to me)

The body requires many different vitamins and minerals that are crucial for both development and preventing disease. These vitamins and minerals are often referred to as micronutrients. They aren't produced naturally in the body, so you must get them from your diet.

If your food is lacking in adequate nutrition it is **very difficult to feel properly satisfied.** Stephen O'Rahilly, Professor of Clinical Biochemistry and Medicine at Cambridge University states that, "People talk about feeling full, but that's not actually what they are feeling as the stomach capacity is huge. The feeling of fullness, usually generated in the brain, is a response **not to food volume but nutrients**. The gastrointestinal tract registers the contents of food we consume, then produces different 'anti-eating' hormones which travel to the brain and trigger a feeling of fullness."

Even if you're eating sufficient calories, or too many calories, you may still suffer severe binge cravings as your body cries out for what it needs. Mere bulk (such as eating four packets of rice cakes) will never satisfy us and we'll still feel hungry. And in the words of Doctor Mark Hyman, "When your body doesn't get the right nutrition, **it just keeps asking for more food**. The endless cycle of craving is a catch-22; people are eating more, getting fatter, but still not feeling satisfied - it's a nightmare from which they can't escape." (*How Malnutrition Causes Obesity*).

Lots of people determine the healthiness of food based on its calorie content alone, but doing so can mean missing out on essential nutrition, which in turn plays havoc with your health. Many so-called healthy foods are so low in calories and nutrition that you'll find it almost impossible to satisfy your appetite, no matter how much you eat. You can fill your stomach with these foods but your body will still be crying out for more.

It may surprise you to know that many recent studies have even linked obesity with severe malnourishment. **You can be overweight or obese and your body can still be starving!** I know this can sound a little crazy, considering obese people tend to eat a lot of food, but they problem may lie in the fact that they are not getting **the right type of food**.

Not only do we need nutrition, but new research shows that we also need to eat a wide variety of food to feel properly satisfied. Experts think we may have evolved this way to ensure we have a nutritionally balanced diet. It would be bad for the human race if we discovered a nice, new food and wanted to eat only that, as no single food is nutritionally adequate for survival. Nutrition is not simply a matter of calories in versus calories out. We need a **variety of nutritionally dense** foods to satisfy our body's biological needs.

There's something else that we really should keep in mind here: not feeding your body the right foods can actually make you feel miserable. Studies show that nutritional deficiencies can cause a whole host of unwanted mental side effects such as depression, anxiety, low mood, low energy, sore muscles, irritation, insomnia … the list goes on.

Really, what we need to keep in mind here is that nutrition is important. If you're not feeding your body the right nutrition, you're going to feel miserable and your body is just going to keep asking for more food.

The nutritional deficiency trap

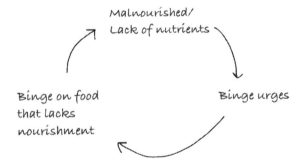

Malnourished/
Lack of nutrients

Binge urges

Binge on food
that lacks
nourishment

NUTRITIONAL DEFICIENCY TRAP BINGE EXAMPLES

The specific cravings binge

When you're having a strong craving for one particular type of food, for example, "I need cheese. Right now!". It may be a sign that you are lacking a particular nutrient.

The never feel satisfied binge

If your not giving your body the right nutrition it just keeps asking for more food. It feels like you can just eat, eat and eat and never reach the point where you feel satisfied.

HOW TO BREAK FREE FROM THE NUTRITIONAL DEFICIENCY TRAP

Food today is too complicated - all you need to do is flip around a packet of something and look at the list of ingredients to see that. Whatever happened to simplicity? It's time to get back to simple, real food.

In terms of the types of food to eat, I would suggest trying to **eat more fresh whole food** as it comes from the earth. This is food as close to it's natural form as possible. Foods that are whole and were once alive. Foods that have been minimally processed or refined. These foods tend to be **packed full** of nutrition. They contain the vitamins, minerals, probiotics, proteins, carbohydrates and fats that go a long way to satisfy and nourish your body.

It's sometimes easy to view our body as a trash chute - where we simply throw any sort of food in and out it comes digested. But, it's not like this at all. What can help is for us to begin to respect our digestive systems, it's not a pipe or funnel for food in, food out. It's our diamond, it's the hub of our entire health and wellbeing. So, let's start nourishing it. We need to start eating more nutritionally dense whole foods.

A simple tip is to try to buy more of your food from the fresh food section of the supermarket. Or, to think about the type of food your great-grandmother would have eaten.

The following are just a few examples, all of which can be easily bought at your local supermarket.

- Grains – Wheat, wholegrain rice, quinoa, bulgur wheat, rolled oats, faro and barley.
- Beans and legumes – lentils, kidney beans, lima beans, split peas, chick peas
- Nuts and seeds – peanuts, almonds, cashews, sunflower seeds, linseeds, pumpkin seeds
- Fruits and vegetables – all of them!
- Eggs

Try eating a well balanced meal containing whole foods and just notice how much better you feel afterwards. You will notice a difference. Your body will instantly recognize the quality of the food. You will experience a deeper sense of satisfaction and contentment from the meal.

To begin with, choose whole foods that you enjoy the taste of. This will make the transition to eating more whole foods a lot easier.

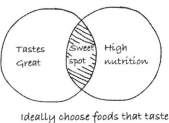

Ideally choose foods that taste
great and are high in
nutrition.

There is no need to get caught up on specific foods, or to make this into an exact science. We don't need to worry about the nutritional content of an apple versus the nutritional content of a cucumber. Just aim to **add more real, whole foods into your diet**. That's all.

Also, please don't make this into a restriction-based rule. I'm not saying that foods with a lower nutrient content are bad and too be avoided. Really, with this program you can eat whatever you want (seriously).

Don't think of this as cutting out foods, think of this as **adding more** nutritionally dense foods to your meal plan. Remember, this stage is all about giving your body everything it needs, **not taking stuff away from it**.

Also, do not think of these suggestions as "diet rules" think of them as guidelines to be followed loosely.

———

Supplements

The stresses, toxicity and diminished nutrient content of food in our modern lives make supplementation a good idea. Vitamins and minerals are essential to your body's capacity to properly digest, stop inflammation, use macronutrients, stabilize mood, think clearly, strengthen biofeedback, heal your gut, balance your biochemistry and much more. Proper vitamin and mineral intake can also dramatically reduce cravings and therefore binge urges (Dr. Cass, H. 2010). Please speak to your doctor before taking any supplementation.

As a start I recommend that you find and take good quality version of a **daily multivitamin** – This is a great place to start. A broad-spectrum multivitamin is key in the smooth functioning of your biochemistry. Quality does make a difference here, so make sure you source a recommended brand.

If you wish to take things further you may also be interested in the following supplements:

Magnesium – I love magnesium and I instantly notice a difference whenever my supply runs out (and I've forgot to order a new batch). My muscles feel stiffer, I'm more tense and anxious than usual, my yoga practice isn't as strong. Magnesium really is a bit of a wonder supplement and is fantastic for reducing stress hormones in your body, while also boosting serotonin (the feel good chemical). It's exceptionally effective for anxiety issues. Studies have shown that a good quality magnesium supplement can reduce food cravings, increase energy and promote better sleep. I recommend buying a **good quality** magnesium citrate, hydroxyapatite, or gluconate. If you haven't tried it out, give it a go. You will notice a difference.

Omega 3 (fish oil) – 99% of people are deficient in Omega 3 fatty acids (Dr Hyman, M. 2010). Omega 3 helps promote the secretion of leptin, which in turn boosts metabolism and improves your body's natural ability to regulate food intake. It has also been found that regular intake of Omega 3 promotes a healthy body weight. When taking a multivitamin and supplementing with Omega 3 at the same time it's important to be mindful of the Vitamin A and D content (which tends to be quite high in fish oil supplements). Read the labels carefully to ensure that you are not exceeding the recommend dietary allowance for each vitamin. If in doubt please consult your doctor who can help you to regulate your supplement intake in a safe way.

Vitamin D – Vitamin D is essential for your body's absorption of calcium (and hence, bone growth) and it has a major role to play in a healthy mood. Deficiency has been linked to depression, dementia, diabetes, chronic muscle pain, bone loss, autoimmune disease and even some cancers. It's a vitamin that is almost entirely missing from our food supply.

Vitamin B complex (including vitamins B6, B12 & folate/folic acid) – B Vitamins are essential for cognitive function, stable mood and memory and are quickly diminished when you experience any type of stress (Dr Hyman, M. 2010). If your multivitamin contains the RDA's of these vitamins you should not take an additional supplement.

Probiotics – Probiotics are beneficial bacteria that enhance digestion, reduce gut inflammation and reduce food allergies. You want to look for a probiotic that has as many different strands of good bacteria as possible, to increase the diversity of beneficial flora in your gut.

Are you able to absorb nutrients?

Some people have moderate to severe digestive issues, which can lead to malabsorption issues. They are unable to adequately absorb important nutrients. This can occur in conditions such as celiac disease, Crohn's disease, lactose intolerance and intestinal damage. If you think you have digestive issues it's vitally important to speak with your doctor and work with a trained medical professional to help remedy the issue.

NUTRITIONAL DEFICIENCY TRAP SUMMARY

Start taking a high quality daily multivitamin. Aim to add more real, whole foods into your diet. You know, fresh vegetables, fruits, beans, whole grains, nuts, seeds and lean animal protein like fish, chicken and eggs (the type of food your great-grandmother would have eaten). This will help you feel REALLY satisfied after eating.

A QUICK RECAP OF THE 3 KEYS COVERED SO FAR...

The Diet Trap, the Blood Sugar Trap and the Nutritional Deficiency Trap solution can be boiled down to one sentence. **Eat enough nutritious, balanced food, spread throughout the day.** That's it in a nutshell.

These 3 keys all focus on balancing your body. This is essential. You must physically balance your body to break free from binge eating. Make this your primary focus to begin with. Start working on these 3 keys first and foremost. Following these keys you can expect **a massive reduction** in your binge urges and a big boost to your wellbeing.

```
┌─────────────────────────────────┐
│                                 │
│        4: THE HABIT TRAP        │
│                                 │
└─────────────────────────────────┘
```

We've already looked at how the your physical body can get trapped into a cycle of bingeing, next let's look at how your mind can become trapped too. This is to do with the way our brains work. This can happen to **anyone** on the planet, so there is no need to take this personally. It is not an indication that your mind is weak or faulty in any way!

The two traps we are going to look at are The Habit Trap and The Food Rules Trap.

Lets start with the **The Habit Trap.**

———

TRAP 4: THE HABIT TRAP

Of course my emotions were to blame. It made perfect sense. Every time I felt miserable I would want to binge. Any intense emotions or uncomfortable feelings would spur the desire to binge on lots of food. Faulty emotions = binge eating. Simple.

The solution in my mind was obvious. Fix my emotions and then my binge urges would be removed. So, I read self-help books, used self-hypnosis techniques, journaled endlessly about my broken feelings and chanted positive mantras. All in the vain hope that it would make me feel better about myself and therefore remove the urge to binge on food. And yes, if I was lucky, sometimes it would work for a day or two but then the old behaviors would come rushing back. Inevitably I would just get angry with myself for not being happy enough. Which in turn just made me more miserable and kind of defeated the purpose of the whole exercise.

For years, I had convinced myself that if I could just feel better about myself, it would somehow remove the urge to binge on food. But then one day this simple fact struck me like a bolt out of the blue. Other people experience negative emotions too. Other people feel sad, other people feel like they're not good enough, other people feel miserable. So why don't they feel compelled to binge on food too? What was so different about me? Were my negative emotions more intense? Did I feel emotions differently than everyone else? I didn't think so. So, I began to research further to figure out what was really going on.

I discovered that research shows that certain foods, especially those with high sugar and fat combinations (e.g. ice cream, chocolate, donuts, cakes and pies) produce "feel good" chemicals like serotonin, dopamine and other endorphins in our brains. Endorphins are powerful, natural opiates that allow you to experience pleasure, a reduction in pain and lower levels of stress. Bingeing on food causes a flood of endorphins to surge through your brain which can temporarily infuse you with a sense of numbness or euphoria - a temporary "high" that triggers the reward regions in your brain. In fact, MRI brain imaging studies have shown that sugar and "junk foods" flood our brains with dopamine and endorphins, stimulating the same areas as hard drugs such as cocaine would.

This can make you feel good… **for a short period of time.** The thing to understand here is that these **highs are temporary,** they do not last. Plus, additional research shows that the feelings of disgust and self-hatred associated with binge eating completely **cancel out any positive affect** for most people.

So now our understanding of binge urges gets a little more complex. The first time that you binged on food it was most likely due to semi-starvation or malnutrition. But then as the cycle of binge eating continued, your brain learns that bingeing on food provides a temporary release from uncomfortable emotions and feelings (a temporary emotional band aid).

The next time you feel an uncomfortable feeling or emotion, **this can trigger the binge urge.** As a result of repeated use, the neurological pathways that link emotional pain with it's "relief" through bingeing, become super-highways.

The process is usually something like this:

1. There is a trigger. Something happens that you don't want to happen (e.g. someone treats you badly).
2. You get upset, or suffer in some other way.
3. You binge on food and your attention is temporarily diverted away from whatever discomfort you're feeling.
4. You unconsciously teach your brain that bingeing makes a specific situation easier or a part of your life more bearable.

As this habit becomes more ingrained, more and more often **you binge on food in response to emotional discomfort and pain**

This type of binge urge is automatic and it comes from the unthinking part of your brain that reacts automatically based on instincts and habit, rather than logic and reason.

There's nothing wrong with this psychological process. It's an important part of being able to function. We use it all the time, when we drive a car or when we brush our teeth. Autopilot behavior like this is learned by repetition and sits in our subconscious, ready to be put into action, without thinking, whenever we need it. This is fine as long as the behavior benefits us and moves us toward the things that we need. The problem occurs when the behavior is maladaptive, when it takes us away from the things we value and starts to create more problems than it solves.

So, this is what you really need to keep in mind:

Yes, negative emotions may trigger a binge urge, but they are **not responsible for the urge**. Non-binge eaters who are perfectly healthy still experience negative thoughts and feelings, yet they do not experience any binge urges in response to these feelings. This is because their brains have not been **conditioned** to do so.

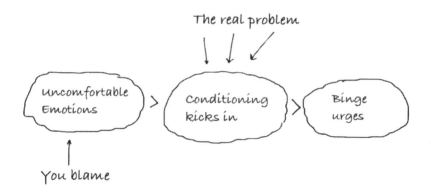

Stop blaming your emotions

Blame the habitual conditioning, not the emotions. If we blame our emotions, then this can lead us to think that our emotions are somehow wrong or faulty. I don't believe that they are. Emotions alone do not make you want to binge. It's only when emotions are connected with conditioned habitual responses that you experience the urge to binge.

"But if I focused on being happier wouldn't I stop bingeing?"

Really? Perhaps if you felt happier you might be in a better place to resist the binge urges. Your willpower might increase, you might feel somewhat stronger when it comes to holding off from giving in to the binge urge for a while. But that doesn't mean the binge urges would go away. If you are stuck within the binge traps the binge urges will always remain. Ready to strike at any moment. Waiting for you to show weakness. This is not real recovery. **It's not real freedom**.

Also, if you hold onto the misguided belief that happiness will help you to stop bingeing you can put yourself under a lot of unrealistic pressure to "just be happier". Paradoxically this drive to be happier can in fact make you more miserable. Whenever you do experience a negative emotion (which is inevitable) you may beat yourself up for "not being happy enough". It's like adding misery on top of misery. There is no need to strive to be happy all of the time in order to overcome your binge eating.

In short, emotions are messy and they're often tough to cope with. This is true for everyone. So, do yourself a favour and go easy on your emotions. **It's not their fault**. They are not responsible for your binge urges. "Fixing" your emotional issues isn't a necessary part of breaking free from binge eating.

"But I am currently living with emotional pain"

If you have had a past trauma or you are currently living with emotional pain, it can have a huge impact on your life. The emotional significance is not to be downplayed. Dealing with emotional pain and trauma is very challenging and we need all the help, comfort and support we can get. But we need real help and support. We need real friends. Not the False Friend of binge eating. **Binge eating only offers the illusion of comfort**. In reality it is slowly destroying your life.

Bingeing on food doesn't support you emotionally, it just temporarily blocks the problem from your mind only to have it rush back afterwards, more intense than ever.

Anything can trigger the conditioning... not just emotions.

It's not just emotions, these types of conditioned cravings can also occur when we've come to associate a certain environment, situation or person with eating.

I used to get cravings whenever I went to my mother's house for Christmas. This was because I had come to strongly associate her house, Christmas decorations and that festive context with being fed a lot of food. But it was also because my relationship with my mum had been emotionally tricky in the past. So the holiday, the environment and time spent with my mother would automatically make my mind think of food and tell me I was hungry when in reality it was just a habitual response.

HABIT TRAP BINGE EXAMPLES

The contextual binge

"I always binge when I visit my Mom." or "I always binge after a tough day at work." Sometimes we can get stuck on a situation or setting trigger. Whenever we find ourselves in that situation or setting it can trigger a binge purely because of the context.

The habitual binge

You just binge, because well, that's what you normally do at this time of day. It's a habit. It's a routine. It's automatic. You may have been doing it this way for so long that to do anything different would feel strange.

The out of the nowhere binge

Something unexpected happens that triggers a binge urge. Someone is rude to you at the store checkout, your boss called you in over the weekend to work, you're just having one of those days and the next thing you know you are in full on binge mode.

HOW TO BREAK FREE FROM MIND CONDITIONING

If the binge urge is a conditioned habit you may have a clear idea of when and where you tend to binge; what series of circumstances "sets off" the automatic habit. Now, you need to work on breaking the habit.

Think about when and where this situation tends to arise and plan to **do something different**. Mix up your routine, change things around so you don't have the same associations. It's a simple strategy but it can be very effective.

If you always buy binge food on your way home from work, drive home a different way that avoids the store. If you always binge in the evening then plan to go out for a walk during that time instead. If you always binge when you are feeling anxious try using the Muscle Release technique instead.

Think about your own personal situation and then schedule in an alternative activity to replace the binge behavior. It takes roughly 30 days of repeating the new behavior to replace the old conditioning and to install it as your new habit. Just stick with it and over time you will notice a big reduction in those habitual binge urges.

Zen10 unexpected binge cravings

Life can always throw us a curve ball when we least expect it. You get into a row with your partner, you discover you were left out of a friends get together, you dent your new car. Emotions ignite and the habitual binge urge kicks in. These binge urges tend to come on suddenly out of the blue. They are a habitual response. The intense emotions and binge urge are intimately entwined, so much so, that it can almost feel like one thing, rather than two separate events.

When these unexpected curve balls arise, it is best to utilize the Zen10 technique. Speed and urgency are helpful here. Don't debate it, don't question it, just apply the technique as soon as you notice the urge.

1. When you notice you are craving a binge urge immediately say the phrase "Zen10" to yourself.

2. I recommend you use the Muscle Release Technique, to help squeeze the tension out of you. Take a very deep breath in and hold it. Tense every muscle in your body for 5 seconds. Release every muscle as you slowly exhale. Rest for 10 seconds and then repeat 3-5 times.

Doing this will help cultivate a space between the intense emotion and the binge urge. You will see that they are two separate entities. One does not necessarily relate to the other. Rest your mind in that space. Dismiss any binge urges. Brush them off and let them be. You can use mental visualization to strengthen your resolve.

3. Wait 10 minutes before taking any action towards a binge. By delaying 10 minutes you give the intense emotion time to subside, so you feel more calm and in control. When the time is up, see if you can extend it by another 10 minutes. Try to keep going until the urge subsides.

Each time you do this, you weaken the habitual conditioning and help to rewrite the brain. Eventually the Zen10 technique will become your new habitual response, your new go to whenever life throws you a curve ball.

THE HABIT TRAP SUMMARY

If you have a clear idea of when and where you tend to binge, break the habit by mixing up your routine and doing something different. For unexpected binge urges that are triggered by an emotional event utilize the Zen10 technique. Each time you do this, you weaken the habitual conditioning.

5: THE FOOD RULES TRAP

There's a general assumption that people who binge on food don't know what they should be eating, that they have no understanding of health and nutrition. But I knew everything about nutrition while I was still bingeing. I'd read every diet, every "don't eat this" list, every article on foods for a flatter stomach. I consumed nutritional "studies" in magazines and scanned nutrition labels at an even greater rate than I consumed food during a binge.

The problem was that every day there'd be a new fad, a new diet rule, a new weight loss expert and all of them had conflicting advice. It got to the point where I was terrified of food - every time I ate something I knew I'd find it on a list of "things you must never eat" the very next day.

And that's the problem.

We want to eat healthy, we really do, so we try our best to follow these rules. Over time, as we encounter more food rules they get added to our list and the amount of acceptable foods we allow ourselves to eat shrinks.

In the beginning our food rules were supposed to make us happier, healthier and more in control. But as time has gone on they've only made us more miserable and even more out of control. We mourn the loss of foods that we don't allow ourselves to eat. We miss the flavors and joy of eating the banned foods, so we end up feeling miserable and deprived.

It's human nature. We always desire what we can't have. If you tell a child that they can play with any toy except the red truck, guess what toy they will want to play with? The same happens with food. When we tell ourselves we "can't" eat certain foods, they become extra special, tastier and more desirable.

In the Ancel Keys Starvation Study, participants were put on a restrictive diet of 1,600 calories per day for 6 months. As the men become more deprived of food, they also became more obsessed about food. They spent their days collecting recipes, their conversations tended to revolve around food and they even noticed a surge in food-related dreams. That's right, even when sleeping they could not escape their obsessive thoughts!

Likewise, the more you deprive yourself the more obsessed you become. Your heightened state of awareness means you suddenly notice that temptation is everywhere. You meet a friend for coffee and you can't take your mind off the abundance of baked goods behind the counter. You take a trip to the grocery store only to find yourself instantly overwhelmed by the smell of freshly baked croissants. You go home, turn on the TV and are immediately bombarded by fast food commercials. Nowhere is safe anymore.

Eventually all that constant temptation wears you down. It erodes your willpower and leaves you feeling vulnerable. Something happens and your resistance falters. Your boss is inconsiderate at work, your partner is in a mood with you, they got your coffee order wrong at the drive-thru or you simply feel like celebrating the weekend. Really, it could be anything.

In that moment, your resolve is gone and you find yourself reaching for your kid's leftovers, or rushing out to the store to buy a forbidden food in a moment of "weakness".

You tell yourself you'll just eat a little but as soon as you take one bite, that's it, a rule has been broken and you are no longer successfully on a diet, or "being good". You believe you have failed and so "all or nothing" thinking kicks in. You find yourself thinking, "I've blown it now, I might as well keep eating," and so you begin to binge uncontrollably. "I'll start again tomorrow," you think. But tomorrow never comes because you can't seem to escape the cycle of binge eating, no matter how hard you try.

The truth is this simple act of breaking a food rule can snowball into a daylong binge fest. Here's the reality. Any diet that demands you give up your favorite foods is not only ridiculous but unsustainable. Who wants to live like that? You are not the problem here, your food rules are!

Studies show that when we eat foods that do not align with our food rules or what we consider to be "good", it tends to **lead to overeating and binges**.

One study looked at the eating behaviors of two groups of people - those who lived by strict food rules and those who did not. The researchers in this study asked individuals from each group to consume a high calorie milkshake, after which they could eat as much ice cream as they wanted. Those who followed strict food rules in their everyday lives went on to **eat significantly more ice-cream** after drinking the milkshake. The researchers hypothesised that this was because they felt they had already failed by **breaking** their food rules and so they continued to overindulge (Herman & Mack, 2975).

Not only that but the amount of guilt we feel about eating certain foods can impact on how much we eat. Participants in another study were asked to consume either a milkshake or a serving of cottage cheese (both containing the same number of calories) before going on to eat as much ice-cream as they liked. Those who initially consumed the milkshake went on to eat considerably **more ice-cream** than those who initially ate the cottage cheese, even though the calorie content was identical! The researchers suggested that individuals with strict food rules experienced **more guilt** after consuming the milkshake because they believed it to be a "bad" or forbidden food. They suggested the **guilt experienced** as a result of having the milkshake triggered the **urge to continue eating**.

This shows that any time we set strict food rules we are only setting ourselves up for failure. The more we restrict food, the more likely we are to binge (Holmes et al, 2014). Eventually our food rules, the very things that were supposed to keep us safe, **will lead us to overeat and binge**. As long as we have food rules we will be driven to break them and will always be stuck in the Food Rules Trap.

FOOD RULES TRAP BINGE EXAMPLES

The all or nothing binge

You've eaten one cookie too many. You think to yourself "Well, that's it. I have blown it now! I might as well eat the whole packet!".

The trigger food binge

This is where eating particular types of food can trigger a binge. These foods can hold a lot of power over you and eating them can cause a lot of anxiety and stress. You've come to associate them with bingeing and they can stir up those urges.

The guilty binge

You've ate something that breaks one of your food rules. You're racked with guilt. You feel miserable and weak. So you binge on food to block out the uncomfortable feelings.

The social pressure binge

You're at a dinner party, BBQ, or social occasion and you experience pressure to eat trigger foods that make you feel uncomfortable. The stress, anxiety and guilt associated with eating those foods leads to a binge.

HOW TO BREAK FREE FROM THE FOOD RULES TRAP

Let's not waste the rest of your life obsessing over what you "should" and "shouldn't" be eating. Food rules don't work. They make you miserable, deprived and prone to binge eating. That's no way to live. It's time to step away from the damaging, rigid "healthy eating" food rules and to begin forming a brand new understanding of what it means to eat in a healthy way.

Realize that in life very few things are as simple as black or white. Most situations have a lot of grey areas. In truth, there is no such thing as "junk" food, "rubbish" food or "bad" food. These are just labels created by the latest so called expert or diet guru. Chocolate isn't necessarily "bad" and apples aren't inherently "good".

Instead, a healthier and more realistic way to view food is: "sometimes food" and "all the time food". Because, ideally, you should eat certain foods more frequently than others. For example, eating foods like fruit and vegetables, meat/tofu, bread/rice/potatoes/pasta and oils each day, will promote good health, so we call these "all the time foods". While other, more energy-dense foods like chocolate, ice-cream and chips should be eaten less frequently and can be thought of as "sometimes foods".

A "sometimes food" is food that you may have avoided in the past or a type of food that you might have only eaten when binge eating. A "sometimes food" may even be one of your favorite types of food or perhaps it's a food that you tend to crave a lot of the time.

What you need to do

Start to introduce "sometimes foods" into your meal plan. When adding a "sometimes food" into your meal plan I highly recommend that you start slowly. Take small steps and go at your own pace. Then, over time, build up to including one or two portions of "sometimes food" into your meal plan every day. The goal here is to destigmatize the food so that it loses its power over you. Keeping that goal in mind, you can decide for yourself how often and when you will choose to eat your "sometimes food".

Start with small portions at first. Perhaps eat your "sometimes food" as a snack. Or alternatively, have it as a portion of a larger meal. If you're worried that eating a "sometimes food" could lead to a binge, try to buy small quantities of the food. That way even if you want to binge on it, you won't be able to. If this is not possible it is wise to throw away any leftovers immediately, before you can be tempted to binge on them.

COACH CORNER

Chocolate used to be one of my main trigger foods, so rather than eating it on its own, initially I would have a little bit with oatmeal for breakfast. When it came to eating pizza (another big trigger food of mine) I would have just one slice and then eat a salad with it, because I knew this would help me to get used to eating it without feeling very overwhelmed.

When I couldn't buy small quantities of my trigger food, I would first throw away the excess food and then eat my meal. I used to feel so awful doing that. I'd grown up my whole life understanding how truly awful it was to waste food and there I was throwing it away. But I had to, it was the only way I could keep myself safe.

Catherine Liberty

Why do I have to do this?

It's not the food itself that leads to a binge; **it's the anxiety, guilt and fear associated with eating the food**. By avoiding specific foods completely you're only reaffirming this anxiety, guilt and fear. By confronting this fear, you'll expose it as fake and then these foods will quickly lose the dread attached to them.

Regular consumption of forbidden foods will prevent you from bingeing on them. You'll no longer feel so deprived and miserable. You'll start to find that prohibited foods lose their sparkle. Previously off-limits foods that are tasted every day are said to not taste as good as imagined. Very soon, it will become evident that you can handle all foods and that they have no control over you.

Try not to think of "sometimes food" as special treats to be eaten occasionally. They're not special and they're not treats. Do not make them more significant than they really are or allow yourself to see them as a reward.

"But what if I want to eat only healthy foods?"

Food recommendations that you may read in magazine articles, etc., are not meant to be taken to the extreme. "Eat more of this and less of that" does not mean "eat only this and none of that". People can easily read recommendations and warp them into what they think to be true.

To be perfectly healthy you do not need to eat perfectly

A varied diet is recommended by health experts. The healthiness of your food intake is best assessed by looking at the overall picture. It is about balance, variety and developing a non-restrictive, non-judgmental eating attitude.

"But, I've been avoiding these foods for years, how can you expect me to just start eating them again?"

Although you may have been trying to avoid these foods, **that has probably not stopped you from bingeing on them.** It's likely that you are going to eat these foods anyway, whether you try to avoid them or not. Would you rather have lots of candy all at once, or some small pieces of candy that you can enjoy, over time, without guilt? There is nothing to fear, trust that your body can handle it.

I'm aware that some methods advocate avoiding certain foods for life, however I strongly disagree with this. It's just not necessary. In time, you can learn to eat any type of food without feeling provoked.

FOOD RULES TRAP SUMMARY

Let go of your strict food rules. Allow yourself to eat all foods GUILT FREE. View food as "sometimes food" and "all the time food". Avoid feeling deprived by eating a portion of "sometimes food" regularly (this also helps remove any anxiety, guilt or fear associated with the food).

6: THE FALSE FRIEND TRAP

Now we are going to explore the last two binge traps, The False Friend Trap and The Inner Critic Trap. These traps are based around your emotions.

I have left these traps to last as I know that for many, dealing with emotions can be challenging. To begin with, it is really best to focus on applying the first 5 keys. That way you give yourself a really solid foundation before tackling the last two traps. Besides when your body and mind are in balance your emotions tend to feel a lot more stable and manageable.

The important point I want to stress at this stage is that we don't want to 'fix' your emotions or change your emotions in any way. Emotions are messy, complicated and at times uncomfortable and difficult to cope with. This is true for everyone. It's just the nature of emotions. Instead at this stage I want to give you some techniques so you can experience ALL emotions without feeling the need to turn to food for comfort.

Let's get started with the **False Friend Trap**

———

TRAP 6: THE FALSE FRIEND TRAP

In my mind I always had good reasons to binge on food. I was feeling miserable, or I was angry at my boss, or I was just feeling a bit down. In fact, I had an inexhaustible supply of reasons.

Having an uncomfortable emotion that I just didn't want to experience was all the excuse I needed for an all-out binge. I would go into autopilot. Without awareness. I wouldn't even question my behavior. The logic was simple: I felt bad, so I needed my binge fix.

But then the more I thought about it, the more I wondered why I called it my binge "fix"? What exactly was it "fixing"? My emotions? If binge eating was so good at helping me manage my emotions, then why wasn't I blissfully happy and always content? Obviously, something wasn't adding up.

So, I started to question what bingeing on food was actually giving me and I realized the answer was nothing. Absolutely nothing. Nada. Zero. Zilch.

Actually, that wasn't exactly true, it was giving me something. It was giving me feelings of guilt for having to lie to the people I loved, feelings of disgust about my behavior, feelings of anxiety and worry for what my life and my health had become and a general day-to-day sense of misery.

This leads me to the **False Friend Trap**.

Let me ask you, do you ever feel that your binge eating gives you something in return? Perhaps you feel it helps comfort you when you feel overwhelmed, or provides an outlet for stress? Perhaps you feel it gives you control over your life or helps you deal with past trauma or pain?

So many people are convinced that bingeing on food helps them in some way. I call this the False Friend Trap. We've all experienced or know someone who we may consider to be a false friend. Perhaps someone who appears to be nice to your face but secretly says hurtful things behind your back. Perhaps someone who only takes from the relationship and doesn't give back. The same principle applies to the False Friend Trap of binge eating.

An example would be a person who comes home to an empty apartment. They feel lonely, which they don't like. They binge on food. They get a buzz and forget how they were feeling. They mistakingly believe that bingeing on food solves their loneliness, but, in reality, **their loneliness remains**.

Bingeing on food then becomes a coping mechanism, a comfort blanket of sorts. This is why people say bingeing on food "helps me manage my emotions" or "gives me a sense of control" or "binge eating is my friend, it helps to comfort me".

Bingeing on food might appear to work as a short-term fix. Long-term, however, it becomes a **bigger problem** than whatever the emotion or discomfort that was being avoided in the first place. The problem is that bingeing on food **doesn't fix anything.** The original problem always remains and by continually avoiding the problem your confidence in your own ability to cope starts to diminish.

This loss of ability to cope doesn't happen overnight. You didn't wake up one day suddenly needing to binge on food just to get through the day. It was a slow process of avoidance that eroded your confidence bit by bit. When we initially avoid emotional situations by bingeing on food, we feel some relief and that relief from discomfort reinforces our avoidance. The problem is, the longer you avoid emotions, **the greater you fear them.**

Avoidance is a prison. It's a trap. It shrinks and restricts your life. After a while you may begin to wonder how you could ever cope with uncomfortable feelings without your binge fix. It becomes your crutch. Something you feel you need to cope with daily life.

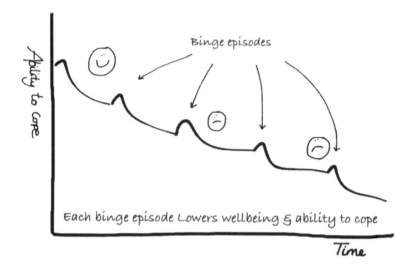

"But bingeing on food helps me cope."

In what way is it helping you to cope? It does not deal with or resolve your issues and it comes at the high price of failed health and an inability to live the life you choose.

What you're really saying is that it **works as a distraction from other problems**. Honestly though, these are problems that wouldn't feel so big if you weren't bingeing on food. When you're living with binge eating, small challenges can seem so much bigger. You may find this hard to believe but it's true.

I understand that this may be difficult to take on board, but it can really help us when we accept **the reality that binge eating gives us nothing**. If we wrongly believe binge eating gives us something, we can feel like we're giving up something of value, or that we won't be able to cope without it.

If you continue to believe that your binge eating serves you in some way it's going to make it much more challenging to break free. You're going to mourn the loss and feel like you're missing out. You might start having pangs for just one more binge.

Think of it this way; could you convince someone to become a binge eater? If you had children would you encourage them to be binge eaters?

"Come on kids, it takes your time, energy and health, you will lose your self-esteem, confidence, zest for life, but I think it's a great coping mechanism!"

Can you see how detrimental these excuses are and how much your thinking has been distorted by binge eating?

"I always thought binge eating was my crutch. I thought I couldn't cope with life without it. The Binge Code has taught me that I can cope so much better without bingeing. The idea that it actually helps you to cope with life better is just an illusion, it makes things so much worse. Now I have energy, time, patience and understanding and now I am emotionally stronger than I've ever been."

Angela M

So, it's time to let go of the idea that you find comfort in binge eating. Let go of the notion that it gives you anything at all. We need to let go of the illusion that bingeing on food helps us cope in any way. It doesn't. **In the long run it just reduces our ability to cope.**

FALSE FRIEND BINGE EXAMPLES

The "I'm alone/bored/sad" binge

When you're feeling a really uncomfortable emotion and you just want to escape into a food-coma to avoid thinking or feeling right now.

The 4hr slow binge

When you're are on the sofa, vegging out, in a comatose state, slowly devouring numerous boxes of chocolates, crisps and sweets over a 4 hour period.

Binge grazing

When you're just picking at foods all day long without any really clear indication of when one meals starts and one meal ends. The whole day is just one big meal.

The planned binge

When you start planning your binge episode hours or even days beforehand. What foods you are going to buy, where you are going to do it, how you're going to sneak away from everyone, etc. As though you are preparing to have a binge as a special treat for yourself.

HOW TO BREAK FREE FROM THE FALSE FRIEND TRAP

When you are feeling emotionally vulnerable you may crave a binge on food for comfort. Realize that this type of craving is not a sign that you're weak or lack willpower. This is simply the part of you that is looking to ease the discomfort you feel. This part of you really has your best interests at heart. It wants to make you feel better, it is trying to protect you. It's your friend, if a somewhat **misguided** friend.

This part of you is like a scruffy dog that's been left out in the rain all day. It's tired, upset and just wants some comfort, affection and love. It doesn't care about your long term goals, your health, or anything else. It just knows that in this moment it feels upset and it wants to feel better.

Instead of turning to our false friend for comfort, we need to be a real friend to ourselves. Recognize that there is a part of you that is upset and needs some nurturing and love. Understand that a part of you wants to be addressed and heard. Say to yourself, "It's okay. I hear you. I know you've had a tough day. Its understandable that you want some comfort. But I'd like to use a new positive behaviour to replace bingeing."

Nurture yourself

We all need a little tender loving care at times. And rather than waiting for someone else to give us attention and comfort, we need to get into the habit of giving it to ourselves.

It is important we learn to look after ourselves here. We are the captain of our own ship. The good news is that you can nurture yourself in many ways. You could have a soothing bath, watch a good movie, snuggle yourself with a warm blanket and a good book, take a nap, talk to a comforting friend or partner, or cuddle the kids. Whatever you feel would best address your needs in that moment.

Rather than wait until you need to be nurtured and can't think of anything to do, I would suggest making a list of at least 5 things you can do to nurture yourself. Take some time to think of things that make you feel loved, supported and emotionally nourished. This way you'll be better prepared when the time comes and you're feeling emotionally vulnerable or sensitive.

Your list might include:

- Playing an instrument.
- Cuddling your partner / kids / pet / self.
- Wrapping yourself in a blanket & watching a movie or your favorite TV series.
- Making yourself a cup of tea or cocoa and listening to your favorite musician.
- Washing your hair / having a shave / moisturizing your hands.
- Giving yourself a foot rub.
- Reading poetry or watching a comedian online.
- Taking a nap.

Basically, anything that feels like self-care or that your needs are being met. Also don't forget to use the Zen10 technique towards any binge urges you may experience.

COACH CORNER

I found this a challenge to begin with. Initially I wondered if I must have a deficiency within me, or perhaps binge eating was the most special, interesting thing I could do. Then I realized, getting high off binge eating was not a normal way to feel. It was an unnatural high and instead of finding another way to feel it, I was going to have to learn to live without it. So keep in mind you are not seeking an exact replacement for binge eating, because you know it was not natural to have those kinds of feelings.

Catherine Liberty

Four simple ideas to nurture yourself

Here are four simple but powerful ways to begin to nurture yourself:

1. Have an Upgraded Bath

A favorite way of mine to push the pause button is to have an Upgraded Bath. I like it because it's so passive. Just fill a bath with hot water and add some Epsom salts. Then get in and soak for twenty minutes. If you want to enhance your experience, light a candle and put on some quiet, rhythmic music. It is helpful for both relaxation and detoxification.

2. Add little "jewels" to your day.

Here is a great simple tip. At intervals throughout your day add little "jewels". Jewels are little moments where you tune in and have a moment's rest and peace. These moments can be anything you wish. Just think of them as something little - something that you like. A little oasis in your day. You don't have to place huge expectations or formalisation on them and they don't need to take a lot of time. They could be as simple as watching a favorite show or just enjoying some some quiet, deep breathing, time.

COACH CORNER

We often think of these little moments as way too simple to make a difference, but they really do. The important thing to do is to allow yourself to really enjoy those moments, guilt free. Soak into them. Savour them. You deserve it!

Catherine Liberty

---

3. Save your binge money

Take the additional money you would have spent on binge foods and to keep it to one side, allowing it to build up and then spending it on a non-food treat for yourself once a week, or once a month. One of my clients used to get all kinds of different spa treatments and massages with the money she saved. Another chose to buy books and clothes.

4. Listen to The Binge Code Deep Trance Guided Meditation Audio

If you like guided meditations you will love this. I have created a 20 minute guided meditation audio specially designed to reprogram your eating habits at the sub-conscious level. You just need to relax and listen. You can download the Binge Code Deep Trance Guided Meditation Audio here: www.thebingecode.com/bonus. Find somewhere comfortable, put on some headphones and just drift off for 20 minutes.

FALSE FRIEND TRAP SUMMARY

Realize bingeing on food doesn't fix anything. It reduces your ability to cope and becomes a crutch. Something you feel you need to cope with daily life. It becomes a bigger problem than whatever emotion was being avoided in the first place. It's a false friend. Say goodbye to your false friend and instead become a real friend towards yourself. Be there for yourself and recognize at times we all need some nurturing and love.

7: THE INNER CRITIC TRAP

"Ugh, I'm disgusting."

"Why would anyone like me?"

"I'm just not good enough."

"I don't belong here!"

"My thighs are like tree trunks."

"I'm so stupid!"

The thought turns my stomach, but that pretty much sums up how I treated myself every single day for those 10 years I binged on food. The truth is, I got more sympathy when I broke my nose than I ever got the decade I was manically bingeing on food. For years, nobody recognized the pain I was in. Nobody recongnized my suffering. Especially me.

I see this behavior in my clients all the time. People who binge on food tend to be incredibly hard on themselves. They really struggle to find a single positive thing to say about themselves. They feel shame and embarrassment at being "over weight" or "uncontrollable around food". They judge themselves as having a lack of willpower, no self-control and are not worthy of love. The longer the bingeing is present, the worse this gets. Eventually it just becomes second nature, a habit, the new normal and they don't even question it.

The problem is the more negative they feel about themselves the more likely they are to eat to block out uncomfortable feelings and emotions! Being mean to yourself only increases the likelihood that you are going to binge on food. Which in turn only further drives more negative feelings. It's a downward negative spiral.

Learning to treat ourselves well is a cornerstone of the Binge Code philosophy, however for most binge eaters this can pose a real challenge. The big question we must ask ourselves is, why?

I think there are two major reasons for this. The first reason is that part of us believes that it's our fault. There's a deep sense of shame because we feel weak for being susceptible to food cravings.

The second reason is that part of us thinks this behavior is helpful in some ways.

Lets take a moment to explore both of them:

> Reason 1: We are harsh towards ourselves because we believe binge eating is due to a personal weakness.

I get it, it's very unsettling. Watching your body do one thing (binge) whilst your mind wants something else completely (not to binge). It's as though a part of you wants to eat and part of you desperately wants to stop eating.

"Am I mad?" The thought crossed my mind frequently. It would appear like a flash out of the blue to strike cold fear deep into my heart. But I just couldn't make sense of my behaviors. If I wasn't mad, then why was I behaving like this?

Not knowing why you do something can be terrifying.

For example: Scratch your head with your fingers right now. Listen closely to the sound it creates inside you. Now, imagine you don't know what's causing that sound. Wouldn't you start worrying that something horribly wrong was happening to your head?

It's the not knowing *why* that causes the problems.

This can lead to all sorts of problems and it can easily lead you to **"invent"** a reason for why you binge on food. Something, anything, to explain why you do it. You may start to blame yourself. Well I must binge on food because it helps me deal with a past trauma or I must binge on food because of my poor upbringing, weak willpower, or because of x, y and z.

Generally, it boils down to this belief: "**I must binge on food because I believe I am fundamentally broken or faulty in some way. It is my fault**"

I see this all the time. Some of the most amazing people, by all accounts wonderful human beings, who are very often highly successful in all other aspects of their lives, completely convincing themselves that they are "freaks" or "broken" or "deeply flawed" because they binge on food. The reality is they are usually **just stuck within the binge traps**. It is truly such a shame that so many beat themselves up unnecessarily for so long. Eventually this self-punishment becomes so ingrained that it's challenging for people to see themselves any other way. They're convinced that they are flawed human beings.

I personally suspected my upbringing was the root cause of my binge eating. My parents separated when I was young and I was constantly moved around to different schools as a kid. I attended seven different schools over fourteen years (that fact still shocks me a little to this day!). I spent my whole life being labeled as the "new girl". My dad wasn't around much and my mum, although loving, was mostly focused on living her own life. It certainly wasn't an ideal upbringing and in my teenage years I did harbor a lot of resentment towards my parents. I began to wonder if my less than ideal upbringing had somehow affected my mental blueprint. Had it broken me in some way? Maybe that was the reason I needed to binge on food?

It took me some time, but eventually I realized that this line of thinking was dangerous for me. It only served to give me an excuse to continue to binge on food. What was the point of even trying to stop bingeing if I was too broken?

Now, in the wisdom of hindsight, I do suspect that my initial food restriction and extreme diet was a cry for attention. I wanted my mum to notice me. I know, so very cliché. But I was a teenager and that's what teenagers do. However, as the years progressed, my life changed, my relationship with my mum grew closer. I wasn't crying out for attention any longer, yet my binge behaviors continued. The factors that motivated me to restrict my food in the first place were no longer relevant in my life. The reasons why I dieted so severely in the first place didn't matter.

The reason why I was bingeing food was because I was stuck in the seven binge traps. Certain practical steps needed to be taken to escape from the traps and resolving the factors present in my childhood simply would not have helped at that point.

It's time to let go of the "I am broken" excuse. You are not weak, broken or faulty because you cannot stop bingeing on food. **It is not your fault**.

It's important to highlight that I am certainly not suggesting that traumas from your childhood or the rest of your life should be dismissed. If you were previously abused, if you suffer with anxiety, alcoholism or any other condition, then the impact of these realities on your life cannot be brushed aside. I'm not spouting a "get over it"

attitude, or suggesting that you shouldn't acknowledge the depth of the hurt you experience. These things need your careful attention, the gentle support of those around you and often the assistance of a therapist or doctor. What I am saying is that just because you binge on food in **no way** does it mean you are **weak, broken or faulty**.

Imagine a genie appeared and said it could remove all your self-hatred, all your negative self-talk so you would feel much happier in your own skin. "But" the genie explained, "I am not going to change your body, just your mind... Would you like me to grant this wish?"

Honestly, how would you respond?

Think about it... You would probably say no. I know I would have said no when I was binge eating.

If you feel anything like I did, you are afraid to like yourself. Because if you like yourself, you're worried that you'll let go of your strict control, just gorge on everything and turn into a big, fat slob. Right?!

This is because you are using self-hatred as a motivation for change.

A part of you wants to be unhappy about how you look because you believe it motivates you. You believe it keeps you striving and stops you from settling for less from yourself. This also explains why rational arguments don't work against self-loathing.

I could say to you, *"Well, if you continue this way you are going to live the rest of your life unhappy. You only live once. You have only one life. Isn't that a waste?!"*

Or I could say, *"Would you talk to someone else the way you talk to yourself? Of course not. Imagine talking to your daughter or a small child the way you talk to yourself. You'd be horrified!"*

Or, *"Happiness isn't based around looks. It's what's inside that counts."*

But none of that would make a difference. It doesn't matter how true these statements are. You already know these things. You know it's not ideal behavior. You already know that you should not base your happiness on your body image, but you do it anyway, because you are **more afraid of what happens if you don't do it**. This is another trap.

The problem with continuing to use self-hatred, mean self-talk and self-bullying as a method of keeping yourself "in line" is that it leads to feelings of despair. When you falter in meeting your own ridiculous, dictatorial standards it's crushing. The continual abuse of yourself leads to depression, anxiety and a sense of defeat. And where do these feelings lead? That's right, straight to a binge. If we don't learn to care for ourselves one of two things happens: either you rebel against your own tyranny, or you are completely trampled by it. And in both cases, your body and mind drive themselves straight to binge eating in order to deal with the horrible feelings.

So, let's look at this again,

Imagine a genie appeared and said, "I can remove all your self-hatred, all your negative self-talk so you will feel much happier in your own skin... yet you will also be **even more motivated** than normal to work towards the best version of yourself... would you like me to grant this wish?"

Is that something you would be more open to accepting?

I'm hoping this time the answer would be yes.

So, let's look more closely at what we're realizing here:

Being mean to yourself is not great for motivation

Imagine a football team is playing while the entire crowd are chanting at them, "Losers! Losers! Losers!" Do you think the team would be motivated to perform their best? Do you think their spirits would be well placed to bring out their best game?

Imagine you paid a lot of money to go on a weekend retreat to see a high-performance coach and all he did was just berate you. "You are a failure, you're rubbish, you suck!" How inspired would you feel to rise up to your potential after a weekend like that? Do you think that would be time well spent, or would you be asking for your money back?

It's a **myth** that you need to be mean to yourself to be motivated for change. It's a big old lie.

INNER CRITIC BINGE EXAMPLES

The I just don't care binge

You just don't care anymore. About stopping binge eating, about yourself, about anything. You decide to just binge, because… well, Why not? Who cares?

The I am fat/ I hate myself binge

When you get into a downward spiral of negative self talk: "I hate myself", "I don't deserve to be happy", "I'm such a fat pig". You then binge on food just to quiet the mind and to give yourself a moments respite.

The "It's not my fault!" binge

This is when you use an excuse to justify a binge, "It's not my fault I binged, my boss was horrible to me today.".

HOW TO BREAK FREE FROM THE INNER CRITIC TRAP

So then, if being harsh to ourselves doesn't work as motivation, what does? The exact opposite. Being positive towards ourselves is what keeps personal motivation alive. All parents know that you need to positively encourage children to allow them to blossom and grow. Likewise, we can encourage ourselves in the same way to tap into our inner strength to achieve our best.

I'm not exaggerating when I say that what follows may be the most powerful self-help exercise you'll come across. There are a few different versions of this same exercise, but the take I like the most comes from the anxiety expert Barry McDonagh and his book "DARE" (which is easily the best book I've ever read for dealing with anxiety issues). He keeps the exercise so simple and as a result it's mightily powerful.

I LOVE MYSELF MANTRA

In any spare moment you have when your mind is idle, silently repeat to yourself: "I love myself." Repeat it over and over again. Roll it around in your mind like a song that gets stuck in your head. Repeat it as you get out of bed in the morning. Repeat it as you shower, as you cook your breakfast, brush your hair and travel to work.

"I love myself. I love myself. I love myself"

For this to be effective ideally you will want to be saying this mantra to yourself for at least a few minutes each day. If you don't like that phrase you can use "I love me" or "I love you", but stick to whichever one you choose. You want to be repeating the same phrase over and over. You want to let it seep in through mechanical repetition.

"I love myself. I love myself. I love myself."

The next step is… Nothing! That's it! Just that one thing, over and over. You may be smirking thinking this exercise is too simple, too ridiculous. But the thing is that it works. It just does.

The beauty of this exercise is that it doesn't matter whether you believe the sentiment or not. What matters is the repetition. Because when you repeat the words "I love myself" like a mantra, it's such a short, simple phrase that it slips past the filters of your conscious mind. This means that the words "I love myself" are able to slide right into that subconscious level of your mind. The place where your core beliefs about yourself are stored and where it slowly starts to embed itself.

"But I feel guilty and uncomfortable doing this"

Of course you will! This goes completely against your habit of beating yourself up. I would suggest that the more uncomfortable you feel, the more effective you will find this technique in the long run. Be patient with it. Let it's magic unfold over time.

So be prepared to feel some resistance. Perhaps your mind will start listing all the reasons you don't deserve to be loved or that this exercise is just silly and you should ignore it.

"But I feel arrogant, conceited and vain!"

This isn't about being arrogant, conceited, or vain. It's about giving yourself what you need in order to love and serve others better. How can you be there for others if you aren't there for yourself?

It is like the pre-flight safety drill you see before take-off on an aircraft. You have to put your oxygen mask on first before you help your children. You're no good to them if you've passed out from lack of oxygen.

"But I don't have any reason to love myself!"

Ultimately, what you need to realize is that **you don't need a reason** to love yourself and **you don't need anyone to say you deserve it**.

"It's not working for me!"

The catch is that you need to do it consistently over a period of time for it to do its work. So, walking the dog, watering the garden, walking to the shop, mopping the floor, boiling the kettle, tying your laces or washing your face: "I love myself. I love myself. I love myself.".

Try it for a couple of weeks and see if you notice any changes. It's certainly not going to hurt you!

Coach Corner

Emotions are messy, complex and generally uncontrollable. Rather than trying to change or control emotions (which isn't very effective) an easier solution is just to look after yourself better so that you feel better. Nurture yourself, take better care of yourself, cater to your needs and don't be afraid to use the "I love myself" mantra for at least for a few minutes each day. Emotional healing takes time so give yourself space to heal.

Catherine liberty

INNER CRITIC TRAP SUMMARY

Stop blaming yourself for binge eating. It's not your fault. Go easy on yourself. You are not perfect and no one expects you to be perfect. Realize that you don't need a reason to love yourself. Repeat the "I love myself" mantra to yourself for a few minutes each day.

APPLYING THE KEYS TO YOUR LIFE

So, there you have it. Your seven keys to binge freedom. I am hoping that you've had some lightbulb moments along the way. I'm hoping that you are beginning to realize that perhaps your binge eating problem isn't really anything to do with you. **You're not weak, or lazy or crazy**. Your binge cravings are a very normal and natural result of how a typical brain and body work. It's really not your fault!

People often ask me, "What in all your years of coaching, gets the quickest results?". What is the number one thing someone can do to see the biggest turn around? I always tell them, if you want to ensure success you have to make a resolute decision in your mind that you are going to commit to a solution that's proven to work. And then create the time and space in your life to make those changes. That's what makes the biggest difference in the end; perseverance and commitment.

Motivation is fickle. Willpower comes and goes. Perseverance and commitment win.

Build daily habits that allow you to implement the seven keys into your life. Apply the keys each day. Stay focused on the program regardless of any challenges or distractions that come your way. It is worth the effort. Binge freedom lies at the other end.

I wish someone would have shown me these keys when I was suffering from binge eating. It would have saved me from years of suffering. Hopefully it can save you from years of suffering too.

So right now the choice is up to you. You have the keys to break free, it is up to you to take action. Are you going think about it or are you going to do it?

Nothing amazing was ever achieved living in the comfort zone.

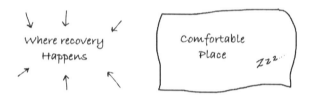

So, let's recap on the seven keys:

THE 7 KEYS TO UNLOCK THE BINGE TRAPS

1. The Diet Trap Key: Under-eating leads to over-eating. Let go of restrictive diets, they don't work. Eat enough food to satisfy your biological requirements. Spread your nutrition throughout the day by avoiding gaps of longer than 3 hours without eating. Try not to graze in-between meals. This will help set a rhythm for your body.

2. The Yo-Yo Blood Sugar Trap Key: Aim to have each meal (and preferably each snack) consist of a ratio of roughly 50% complex carbohydrates, 25% proteins and 25% fats. This will do wonders to stabilize your blood sugar levels and reduce your sugar carvings.

Over time, discover the ratio that works best for you, so you feel fuller for longer and more satisfied after each meal.

3. The Nutritional Deficiency Trap Key: Start taking a high quality daily multivitamin. Aim to add more real, whole foods into your diet. You know, fresh vegetables, fruits, beans, whole grains, nuts, seeds and lean animal protein like fish, chicken and eggs (the type of food your great-grandmother would have eaten). This will help you feel REALLY satisfied after eating.

4. The Habit Trap Key: If you have a clear idea of when and where you tend to binge, break the habit by mixing up your routine and doing something different. For unexpected binge urges that are triggered by an emotional event utilize the Zen10 technique. Each time you do this, you weaken the habitual conditioning.

5. The Food Rules Trap Key: Let go of your strict food rules. Allow yourself to eat all foods GUILT FREE. View food as "sometimes food" and "all the time food". Avoid feeling deprived by eating a portion of "sometimes food" regularly (this also helps remove any anxiety, guilt or fear associated with the food).

6. The False Friend Trap Key: Realize bingeing on food doesn't fix anything. It reduces your ability to cope and becomes a crutch. Something you feel you need to cope with daily life. It becomes a bigger problem than whatever emotion was being avoided in the first place. It's a false friend. Say goodbye to your false friend and instead become a real friend towards yourself. Be there for yourself and recognize at times we all need some nurturing and love.

7. The Inner Critic Trap Key: Stop blaming yourself for binge eating. It's not your fault. Go easy on yourself. You are not perfect and no one expects you to be perfect. Realize that you don't need a reason to love yourself. Repeat the "I love myself" mantra to yourself for a few minutes each day.

Don't forget to apply the **Zen10 technique** to any binge urges!

You can download a printer friendly version of this list from www.thebingecode.com/bonus. Print it out, stick it on your wall where you can see it and start applying the keys to your life.

When starting out, avoid being overwhelmed by implementing one key at a time. Just start with the first key (the diet trap key) and then move on to the next when you have got that one in place. Everyday take a small step forward, give the keys some time to work their magic and within a week or two you will start to notice a dramatic reduction in your binge urges.

An easy way to measure your progress is to track the intensity of your binge urges using the Binge Urge Scale. The scale runs from 1 to 5, with 5 being the strongest and 1 the mildest.

BINGE URGE SCALE

1: Barely noticeable

A passing, fleeting thought. No actual physical desire, with no emotional reaction. Easy to brush off as just a silly thought.

2: A mild craving

Physical sensations are noted. The thought enters your mind. You may feel a slight hunger above the neck. Mild discomfort.

3: A craving

Physical sensations are becoming more pronounced and uncomfortable. Much more challenging to ignore. Experiencing emotional reactions to the urge.

4: An intense binge urge feeling

Feeling uncomfortable. Emotionally anxious, irritated. Feels like it's coming from deep within your core. Harder to think clearly. Fight-or-flight sensation triggered.

5: Super intense urge feeling

Feeling completely out of control. Strong physical sensations, emotionally intense. Feeling jittery. Powerful waves of compulsion. Rapid thoughts, shallow breaths, difficulty thinking clearly, anxious. In a trancelike state.

As you notice a reduction in your binge urge intensity, then you know you are moving in the right direction. Other signs of progress to look for include:

- Less frequent binges
- Shorter binges
- Binges on smaller amounts of food
- The ability to stop / lose interest in the middle of a binge
- Bouncing back more quickly when a binge happens
- Using the Zen10 technique to stop a binge from happening even when the urge is present
- Noticing decreased stress levels around food
- An increased sense of wellbeing and inner peace
- Spending less time obsessing or thinking about food.

Keep in mind that this is not a linear process. Some weeks will be better than others. Don't get upset if you are successful one day, but have a setback the next.

The first thing you may notice when you avoid giving in to a binge urge is a surge in emotions. I know I did. Without the "protection" or "numbness" that binge eating used to give you, every emotion and negative thought is going to feel a little amplified. You may experience an increase in anger, frustration, self-hatred, sadness, but also on the other hand you may experience more happiness and joy too. This is simply your emotions recalibrating themselves and it's a good sign of progress.

It's really helpful to have an idea of what the path to freedom looks like so you're better prepared and know what to expect (but bear in mind that no two journeys look the same!)

The Path to freedom

- The path to freedom is a gradual reduction in your binge frequency, intensity and duration over time.
- The path to freedom is slowly reducing the number of binges you have each week, it's not promising yourself to never binge again.
- The path to freedom is having some weeks which are tougher than others, but having the wisdom to see the bigger picture and to realize you are still making progress.
- The path to freedom is not about wanting a quick fix but understanding it takes time for your body to heal.
- The path to freedom is giving your body time to discover it's optimum, healthy weight that is right for your body type.
- The path to freedom is about doing the best you can and accepting you are human. No one expects you to be perfect and you do not have to be.
- The path to freedom is having some days when you are super motivated and others when you are less so. It's also having the wisdom to realize that this is normal; there is nothing wrong with this.
- The path to freedom is a journey of rediscovering who you are when you're free from the pain of binge eating.
- The path to freedom will have unexpected challenges, new insights, twists and turns, fantastic discoveries, fears to be confronted, beliefs to be questioned and so much more.
- Freedom from binge eating will be one of the best gifts you will ever give yourself!

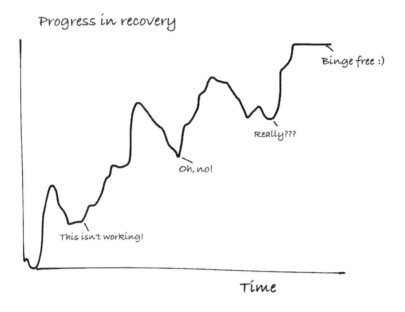

The truth is that the journey to binge freedom is an imperfect road. It has bumps along the way. I know it's seductive to imagine that you are going to be someone who has a perfect journey to binge freedom but the truth is, it just doesn't happen that way. Life is constantly throwing us curveballs and placing obstacles in our way and you need to accept that.

O ne of the biggest challenges with the Binge Code is meal planning. So let's break it down and cover it in detail, so you know exactly how to meal plan for success.

If you are stressed at all about what you are going to eat, I strongly suggest you start meal planning. It can really help alleviate any anxiety that might arise when you need to make food choices right before meal-time when you're feeling hungry.

The key to meal planning is keeping it simple. Especially at the start. Don't worry about gourmet cooking if you're not a great cook. Stick to the basics. If you're not into elaborate sauces or flavors don't worry about them. This is about healing and nourishment. You can worry about being a fancy chef some other time. We're going to start simple and then as we get comfortable with simple, we can work on more elaborate recipies.

Choose a time when you're not hungry and you're not in a triggering environment and create your meal plan.

Decide when you are going to eat.

Include in your meal planning the time of the day when you will eat your meals and snacks (avoiding gaps of longer than 3 hours). Think of this as a general guideline, not a strict rule.

Start with 7 meal recipes

We're going to start by deciding on 7 meal recipes. 2 meal ideas for breakfast, 2 for lunch and 3 for dinner. That's 7 recipes to begin with. If this sounds too restrictive, remember this is just the beginning. Once you're comfortable here you can start to be more adventurous.

Sit down and come up with 2 breakfasts meal ideas, 2 for lunch and 3 for dinner. Use a cook book if you need inspiration but choose simpler, easier to make recipes, that you are comfortable with.

You will want to have roughly half of your plate dedicated to carbs, a quarter dedicated to proteins and a quarter dedicated to fats. Aim to include as much real whole foods are possible in the meals.

Brainstorm a few ideas for snack foods that can easily be grabbed and eaten when you're in a rush. Things like protein bars, fruit and nut/seed mixes are great options as they can be stored easily and they cut out on the preparation time too. Try to get into the habit of having some things you can snack on in your bag/car/somewhere that is easily accessible. I would always carry around some emergency snack foods every time I left the house just in case my day didn't go as planned and I found myself stranded without food.

Check your portion sizes

I just used a plate as my guide. One plate was one meal. With snacks, I generally stuck to things that were "snack sized" and portioned already, like a piece of fruit with a portion of cheese, or a graze snack box, or snack-portioned nuts.

Another suggestion might be to use your hands or fists to determine a portion. Your palm determines your protein portion. Your cupped hand determines your carb portion. Your thumb determines your fat portion.

You should settle on a way to measure portions that is general and is reassuring to you.

If you feel that you need to count calories to avoid a binge, you can do that too. As a suggestion, if you're working with 2,200 calories a day, you can break that down to 500 calories per meal, 230 calories per snack.

Another option is to purchase individual portions from the supermarket (be careful they are the correct size; a lot of the serving sizes in these products are much too small).

Ultimately you don't have to measure anything because dieting, strict portion sizes and counting calories never work in the long run. Try counting and measuring only if you need to for now and stop once you have an understanding of what portion sizes are appropriate for you.

Go shopping

Make a list of everything you need to buy for your planned meals and go shopping. Supermarkets can be triggering environments for many, so before shopping for any foods make sure you're not hungry and you're feeling safe. Make it quick - stick to your shopping list and avoid over complicating things for yourself. Avoid going down the candy lane of your supermarket if this is triggering for you. If it's too much for you, perhaps you can order your food online.

Prep your meals in advance

Preparing your meal in advance can be really helpful.

The oven works well for this. For example you can purchase chicken breasts, some sweet potatoes and extra veg and cook them in the oven. Very simple. Once your food is cooked, portion it out for 5 nights. You may wish to purchase good quality food containers for storing and transporting your food (there are some great BPA free options at Amazon.com).

Lay out the 5 containers for your meals, put some chicken in each one and add in your sweet potatoes and veggies. If you want to add rice or quinoa then do so. Drizzle with olive oil and serve with avocado for some good fats.

Freeze your prepared food and put only tomorrow's meals in the fridge. Take the following day's meals out of the freezer the night beforehand. This helps to prevent you bingeing on your prepared food. Do this with a few meals so you're not eating the same thing each night.

If you don't/won't cook, you can consider buying prepared meals from a company that provides this service or ask a family member or a friend to cook for you. Alternatively, you can just cook the meal whenever it's required. Again whatever works best for you.

Think about tomorrow

Life will always find a way to interfere with the best plans. Be prepared for this. Your plan will always need adjustment or modification in the face of change.

The night before (or first thing in the morning), take 5 minutes to think about the next day ahead. Think about appointments and work commitments, anything that can interfere with you eating your planned meals or snacks. Then troubleshoot some solutions.

For example, a lunch meeting at work where they provide a buffet, how are you going to get around that? Think of what you will eat there, or if you can bring your own food, etc. Perhaps you will need to bring a packed lunch?

Leftovers

If you feel that leftover food may be a binge trigger then I recommend you dispose of your leftover food in the trash as soon as you are finished eating. Some people feel uncomfortable with the idea of throwing food away but it's vital to safeguard your progress in this way. Alternatively, you may want to freeze the food if it is something that you want to keep for another day.

Add a little flexibility

There will be times when, for one reason or another, you just can't stick to a meal plan and that's okay. There's no need to panic. It's okay to allow some flexibility when needed. Even without a plan you can still make food choices that keep you in balance.

"This sounds too strict!"

This can seem quite regimented. However, it is so important to think of your meal plan as your healing plan. You need to eat regular, balanced, whole foods to heal your body. In time, as you get more comfortable with the program, you can let go of the formality and allow your plan to naturally shape into something that works for you.

COACH CORNER

Some people swear by meal planning. They need to have their well thought out meal planned in advance so that they don't relapse or end up binge eating. Whereas others find it a little too intense to plan every single meal and snack in advance. This was the case for me.

I rarely planned out meals ahead of time and instead I bought in lots of balanced, nutritious, groceries each week and also some "sometimes" foods (but not my worst trigger foods). I'd simply stick to my set meal times and then decide what I was going to eat a little before that time.

I avoided my worst trigger foods entirely for a full month to give myself a good head start before dealing with that stress. I also kept moderately triggering foods out of sight at all times (avoiding visual triggers really worked for me) and I only ate moderately triggering foods at "safe times".

I needed around 2200 calories each day. I aimed to eat 500 calories for breakfast, lunch and dinner, splitting the remaining calories between my three snacks. Using the knowledge I already had of calorie content I estimated the calories for each of my meals

I ensured there was some carbohydrate, protein and fat with every meal (and snack). I combined all the time foods with some of the time foods. I'd often eat quite random combinations of foods to achieve this (pizza and salad still to this day is probably one of my favorites).

This worked for me, but with a little trial and error you should discover what works best for you here.

Coach Catherine

Here's how one of my coaching clients planned her meals:

"*Eating every 3 hours-ish has meant I'm not eating late at night, which is great and works wonders for my energy levels, reducing preoccupation with food and weight. I now start my day with a good breakfast and I actually sit down to eat breakfast. It also means I am not eating standing up in the kitchen (which I always did before) or eating in front of the open refrigerator. I measure yogurt, milk, grains, beans, etc. in measuring cups and I use my hand to measure fruit, vegetables and nuts. This works for me as it isn't rigid, but it's a good estimate. I used to restrict in the mornings and then over-eat and/or binge at night, which I no longer do. This is a significant change for me.*"

Food journaling

Recording your food intake is a great idea, even if it's just for a few days each week. This was how I discovered so many insights about myself. It's how I discovered that fruit alone was the absolute worst snack for me (my hunger would skyrocket very soon after). It's also how I discovered the very strong connection between my hormones, my hunger and binge urges (I'd always be on the verge of relapse in the lead up to my period). I've created a special food journal for The Binge Code that you can download here: www.thebingecode.com/bonus.

Here is an example of what it looks like:

Try it out for a few days and see if it works for you. You may find it extremely helpful. I know I did and so have many of my clients.

Visit www.thebingecode.com/bonus to download the Binge Code Food Journal

MEAL IDEAS

To help you get started, here are some sample meal ideas that adhere to the Binge Code principles:

Breakfast Ideas

- A bowl of porridge with a sprinkle of seed mix or nuts
- Cereal with milk or yogurt and fruit, with sprinkle of chia or grounded flaxseed
- Wholemeal/multigrain toast (x2) with a nut spread (almond, peanut, cashew), a small tub of greek yogurt and a piece of fruit
- Wholegrain wrap with bacon, lettuce, avocado slices and tomato
- Scrambled eggs on toast with avocado. Slices of watermelon on the side.
- Turkey rashers fried in a little olive oil with mushrooms and tomatoes
- Baked beans and toasted wholemeal pitta plus 1/2 a grapefruit
- A pancake: 1 egg, a little milk and oat bran mixed together with a fork, fry in a little olive oil.

Lunch Ideas

- Thick soup such as chicken and vegetable or bean and vegetable with a bread roll or some toast
- A bowl of salad with tuna or salmon and nuts mixed into it plus a serving of potato/pasta/couscous/tabbouleh (carbs)
- A sandwich on wholegrain bread or a roll with a slice of meat, egg, cheese and salad (tomato, lettuce, cucumber, carrot)
- 1-2 apples diced, topped with cottage cheese and sprinkled with chopped Brazil nuts. Serve with a large, mixed green leaf

salad decorated with curls of smoked salmon and salad dressing

Dinner Ideas

- Pasta with a tomato-based sauce (include tuna or bacon etc.) served with green vegetables (e.g. broccoli, beans, asparagus) or salad
- Fish/beef/pork/lamb/chicken with salad or vegetables and potato/sweet potato/pumpkin
- Stir fried meat/tofu and vegetables with rice or noodles
- Salmon steak baked in a tinfoil parcel with green beans, almond slivers and garlic/onion to taste. Serve on bed of quinoa cooked in bouillon (stock)

Some Snack Ideas

Snacks keep blood sugar levels balanced throughout the day and they help manage hunger. Preferably your snacks should be high in protein and fat to help stabilize your blood sugar and and to keep satiated for longer.

- Fruit and ricotta cheese
- Dried fruit and nuts
- An apple and a protein bar
- Cheese and crackers
- Veggies and hummus
- Nut butter with apple
- Greek yogurt and some apple slices
- Tinned tuna or salmon with wholegrain crackers
- Protein bar or energy bar

HELP! I BINGED!

"I'll never binge again" or "This stops from tomorrow!". How many times have you made a promise like this to yourself?

Yes of course the primary goal of The Binge Code is to never binge eat again. But in truth, promising yourself that you will never binge again is **actually counterproductive**. If you were learning any other new skill, like skateboarding, can you imagine how absurd it would be to commit to never falling off. You'd fully expect to be wobbly and awkward at the start. You'd expect that though, right?

I can't stress this enough. Having a binge whilst on The Binge Code **doesn't actually mean you've failed** and it doesn't mean that you're back to square one. Just like falling off that skateboard doesn't mean that you're not learning how to skate. Although it can be very upsetting at the time, your progress isn't "undone" if you do slip and have a binge.

We've helped thousands of people overcome binge eating and nearly **all of them relapsed multiple times** and nearly all of them experienced those same fears. They felt devastated and disheartened, but **they didn't give up** and their relapses didn't stop them. **They made it**. They're now binge free.

Path to binge freedom

What people think it
Looks like

What it really
looks like

"I had this very powerful experience where I binged, but before I even left the kitchen I had this "conversation" with binge eating – I told it that it could make me relapse as much as it wanted, but that I was never going to give up. In that moment the fear just left, I knew relapsing couldn't destroy me."

Jo

Forgive yourself

In the meantime forgive yourself for any binge episodes. Forgive yourself, forgive yourself, forgive yourself. An attitude of compassion and forgiveness can go a long way to healing any emotional pain. At the end of the day you are only human, you are embarking on a life changing journey right now.

It is normal to have off days. Days where all you want to do is resist change and where you may find yourself turning back to binge eating in order to escape from difficult feelings and negative emotions and you know what? It's okay to find yourself feeling that way, it's normal and it does not mean you don't have what it takes to break free from binge eating.

Talk to yourself kindly and remind yourself that no one was to blame for this episode. You are human. You are not perfect. You will never be perfect. **No one expects you to be perfect**. So forgive yourself for not being perfect. Besides, lots of people say their relapses are integral to their success.

So, take a moment to fully forgive yourself for any binge episode. It's okay. It really is. Once you really forgive yourself you'll feel freer. You'll feel lighter. You'll have more energy. You can then use that energy and direct it towards a more successful tomorrow rather than dwelling on any setbacks today.

Get back on track

Just because a situation isn't favorable at the moment, it doesn't mean that it is ruined or that things will never improve. Refuse to give in to thoughts that tell you the whole day is ruined and instead take every second of the day **as a new chance to get back on track**.

Try to think of your day in shorter segments (basing it around meal times is a great way to do this). If you have a bad experience in one segment, stay positive and know that with the next meal you can get back on track. This will help you to stop allowing small challenges or contained incidents of over-eating from ruining the rest of your day.

If you are feeling bloated

After a binge episode, if you are feeling overly bloated, get moving. Light exercise is the best thing you can do to help your body bounce back and digest your food. The operative word here is light! Taking a walk can do you a world of good. Not only does it speed up digestion, it'll also even out your blood sugar and clear glucose from your bloodstream.

———

BONUS TIPS

Here are some extra tips to help supercharge your journey to binge freedom.

Get a good night's sleep

Not only does sleep loss appear to stimulate appetite, it also stimulates cravings for high-fat, high-carbohydrate foods. "When you have sleep deprivation and are running low on energy, you automatically go for a bag of potato chips or other comfort foods," says Susan Zafarlotfi, PhD, clinical director of the Institute for Sleep and Wake Disorders in New Jersey. This is not helpful if you're trying to overcome binge eating.

It is important to get a good night's sleep. This is something that I feel very strongly about. Getting enough sleep allows your body to reset each day and does wonders for improving your general wellbeing and increasing your emotional stability. I learned through self-care how important it is for me to get 8 hours of sleep each night. Some people find that 7 is enough for them and others need 9 hours. Each person is different. However, there is an amount of sleep that your body and mind need in order to function at their best.

Get rid of triggers

Starting out on the program, if you know something is a trigger for you it does makes sense to try and avoid it. There's no need to put yourself under unnecessary pressure. However, while it can be helpful to avoid triggers in the short term, in the long term it's not an effective solution.

The problem with trying to remove triggers entirely is that in reality everything and anything could be a trigger: a fleeting negative thought, a television advert, a family member, a Facebook post, feeling bored, etc. This makes it nearly impossible to avoid all triggers.

In saying that, here are some strategies you may find helpful when starting out:

- Spend an hour and go through your house clearing out any potential triggers.
- Studies show we are more likely to eat the first foods that we see, so keep binge foods hidden from view or better still, don't have them in your house at all.
- If you live with someone else and you can't get rid of or hide food ask them if they'd be willing to put triggering foods away, or cut down on how much food they buy.
- Remove any "skinny" clothes that you aspire to fit into.
- Throw out any fashion or health/diet magazines.
- Get rid of anything else that may be a trigger for you.

If you cannot throw anything out, try storing those items away where they will not be seen. Perhaps in your attic or in an outdoor shed. Hopefully you'll find this to be a very liberating and freeing activity.

Get rid of the scales

Weighing scales are one of the biggest binge triggers. It's been proven that both "good" and "bad" scale numbers can lead to binges. If we get on the scale and it says that we've lost a great deal of weight, we can use that as a justification to overindulge. If the scale says we've not done as well as we'd hoped, we can use that as the reason to quit and give up.

Scales are not accurate. Studies show that a fluctuation of plus or minus 1kg (2.2lbs) over consecutive days is common and fluctuations of plus or minus 0.5kg (1lbs) are very common. Weight can fluctuate and vary depending on hormone changes, gains in lean muscle mass, water retention and even whether or not you've used the restroom recently. So, it's definitely time to ditch the scales! You don't need them.

HELP! I AM IN THE MIDDLE OF A BINGE!

E ven if you find yourself bingeing on food you are still on the Binge Code program. You have not blown it! You have not failed in anyway. This is important because I want you to let go of that "black and white thinking". That sense of "Ah well I've blown it now!". Then just letting the flood gates open to consume as much food as you can.

You have not "blown" anything. A big part of my job as a coach is to challenge this "all or nothing" perspective because in truth, progress can happen... wait for it... even when you are in the middle of a binge!

Bring awareness to the binge

In the middle of a binge we often find that we are completely lost in thought. The last place our mind shines any attention on is the actual food we're eating. This state of mind is often referred to as the binge-trance.

But, I think the word "trance" is misleading. It implies that there's nothing going on in your head. That your brain is vacant during a binge. In reality, if you bring your awareness back into your body you'll realize that you were not in a trance but lost in deep thought.

Lost in a constant cycle of worry, planning, remembering, analysing, judging, brooding and comparing. You were daydreaming and not really living in the present moment.

So, we're going to use a little technique to bring your awareness back to the here and now. I call this "The Binge Commentary" technique.

THE BINGE COMMENTARY

If you find yourself bingeing on food, as soon as you can, start a running commentary of what is happening. You can do this out loud or in your mind, whichever you prefer. Describe what you can feel and what you're doing. Describe it in as much detail as you can, as it happens. It may seem ridiculous at first but a running commentary will really help you stay focused and present.

So, it might sound like this: *"I'm grabbing some cookies. I'm putting the first one in my mouth. It tastes very sweet. It's really dry in my mouth. I'm chewing it and it's turning into a sticky paste, but I'm putting another one in now ..."*

As you eat the cookies start paying attention to your jaw, the taste of each bite, the texture. Try to avoid talking about your emotions and instead focus on the physical sensations. What's going on in your body?

I understand it can be quite difficult to talk aloud when eating, but this can also really help to slow down your binge. The more time you have means more chances to become present.

Why do this?

One of the common features of a binge episode is a sense of loss of control. The Binge Commentary is great for regaining control. This simple technique will snap you out of the trance and bring your awareness and focus back to the act of eating. You will be eating, not daydreaming. It will just be you and the food.

By being present and aware, you will start to notice what it really feels like to binge on food. For the first time maybe ever, you will be facing your binge eating behaviours head on. You'll be fully present. You'll be really experiencing it as it's happening to you. You'll no longer be lost in thought. In a way, you will be like a curious observer, mindfully watching yourself during a binge. As a result, **you'll be able to truly witness how a binge really affects you.**

It's easy to be tricked into thinking a binge feels good or does something positive for you. But how do you know? You weren't there mentally while it was happening. It's like buying a ticket to a fairground but never going inside, then telling yourself it's your favorite place on earth. How do you know, when you haven't actually been there? However, by using The Binge Commentary you'll discover what your binge episodes are REALLY like. And this information can begin to **inform how you feel** about "letting" a binge happen.

Things you may notice

Perhaps the first thing you will notice is that binge eating to mask uncomfortable emotions, is far less appealing when you push yourself to remain present and to pay attention to your feelings and behaviours.

You may find this to be a bit of a scary, intense experience. I know I did. You may feel uncomfortable, bored and/or frustrated. Part of you may want to throw your arms up in the air and exclaim that the whole exercise is ridiculous. That's because this part of you doesn't want to look too closely at the binge experience for fear that you will expose the truth – the truth that it is **not serving you** in any way. This is generally because we would rather think about anything other than the reality of bingeing on all these foods we don't allow ourselves to eat.

But this discomfort is a good thing. It is a clear sign that you're beginning to expose the binge for the **False Friend** that it is. You may notice that you don't enjoy the binge as much as you did before. You may find binges do not give you the same level of satisfaction as they once did. That's great! It'll make them easier to let go of.

You may find your food doesn't taste as good after a while. You may notice how things that normally taste really sweet lose the sweetness they had at the beginning. Everything starts to taste the same. You might realize that you don't actually like the taste of some of your usual binge foods (and you'd never noticed before because you'd never paid attention). You may find that when you pay attention to what you're eating you feel full much sooner, which can lead to eating less food and having smaller binges.

"But when I binge I want to be lost in thought!"

If your mind doesn't even want to be present during a binge, **then why are you bingeing on food?** This is a big clue that a binge on food isn't really what you need. Perhaps, what you really need is just a mental break from your worries and stresses. If it's the mental distraction that you want, that's good because there are lots of ways to mentally distract yourself which don't involve eating lots of food; watch a heartfelt movie, get in touch with your creative side, go shopping, watch cute animals fall asleep on YouTube…

"But this takes the fun out of bingeing"

Great! This is exactly what we want as it helps to take away the special appeal of a binge episode. Also, ask yourself why does being mentally present during something take the "fun" out of it?

It would seem to me that if something was enjoyable then we would **want** our minds to be present during the experience. You don't watch a movie so that you can you drift off in thought.

"I keep getting lost in thought"

This is very normal and it is not a sign that you're doing your Binge Commentary wrong. Don't worry about getting distracted. If you're trying to use the Binge Commentary but keep thinking or worrying about something else, pause and tell yourself that it can wait. Tell yourself, *"I'll think about that after I eat, from now on I'm being mindful of my food."*

If you find yourself worrying too much, write your worries down

It can be helpful to create a worry journal. Set aside 10 minutes each day and write your worries into your journal. Thinking about your anxieties and stresses and putting these thoughts down on paper will help you to process them. Then you won't feel the need to process them while your eating.

Aim for an improvement.

Each time you use the Binge Commentary technique I want you to aim for some sort of improvement. Perhaps you could stop your binge much sooner than usual or binge on smaller amounts of food.

Other areas you could work on might be:

- Being less frantic during a binge
- Paying more attention during a binge
- Stopping/losing interest in the middle of a binge
- Eating more nourishing foods during a binge.

———

I've created a special Binge Code audio track which you can listen to if you find yourself in the middle of a binge. You can download it from www.thebingecode.com/bonus.

PART 3

BIOBALANCING™

STAY BALANCED, BINGE FREE AND AT YOUR HEALTHY WEIGHT FOR LIFE

INTRODUCING BIOBALANCING™

Welcome to Part 3 of The Binge Code: BioBalancing™. In this stage we ensure you stay binge free and at your ideal set-point weight for life. Also, as a nice bonus, you'll learn how to live your life to the fullest as you being to tap into your true self.

I must stress, this is an advanced stage of The Binge Code. If you are still experiencing strong binge urges, your body may not be accurately communicating with you its needs and you may find BioBalancing™ too challenging.

If you are just starting out, I strongly recommend you focus on parts 1 and 2 of this book and leave BioBalancing™ aside for now. To begin with, use the Zen10 technique and apply the keys to escape from the binge traps. This is the best thing you can do right now to stop bingeing and get back in balance. Once you've noticed a big reduction in your binge urges and you are feeling much more stable, then you can start BioBalancing™.

Of course you can read through this section and get an idea of what it is all about, but don't worry about applying these principles until you feel ready. I guess the point is to avoid overwhelm and to take your time with the program. Don't bite off more than you can chew!

With that said, let's get into this…

When I started applying the Binge Code keys to my life I began to notice a dramatic reduction in my binge urges. It was working! It was really, really working! This gave me the confidence boost I needed to really push on. I had a few relapse episodes (nearly everyone does) but within six months my binge urges were gone. I felt euphoric. My weight did fluctuate a little, especially at the beginning, but eventually it settled at its natural set point (which I am very comfortable with).

But then the thought hit me. What am I going to do now? I had been bingeing on food for over 10 years. I had been on some sort of diet for over 10 years. It was all I had known. It was then, I realized that I had no idea how to eat like a normal person. Other people made eating look so easy, yet I felt bewildered. With no guidelines, no rules, no plans telling me when, how much and what I should eat, how was I ever going to know when, how much and what to eat?

What was I to do? I knew that I didn't want to stay on a scheduled meal plan for the rest of my life. Yet I was terrified to let go of that safety net, in case I slipped back into my old dangerous food habits that got me into trouble in the first place. Like a little bird's first flight from the nest, worried, cautious, concerned, I took my first tentative steps into the world of 'normal eating'.

Pretty much off the bat I discovered that there is no such thing as 'normal eating'. Well, nothing you can point your finger at and claim as 'normal'. Everyone who is comfortable with food eats to the beat of their own drum. They have their own unique eating pattern. Their own 'normal'.

And that's when I realized that I needed to discover my own 'normal'. The eating pattern that works for me. And I was the only person who could tell me what that was. Yet I was clueless! I had no idea! I felt more lost than ever!

Eventually the penny dropped. I had my eureka moment that changed absolutely everything. It was so clear now. I realized that although my mind had no idea how to eat normally, **my body did**.

What's this all about?

Your body is always communicating with you. A steady stream of subtle feelings, sensations and feedback constantly informing you of its current state. The big question is, are you listening?

Most of us are chronically out of touch with our own bodies. Some of us like to ignore the fact that we even have a body. In general, we are so busy rushing around doing things, we spend so much time trapped in our own head (the prison without walls) that we never really become aware of how our body feels. By continually ignoring the needs of your body you weaken your connection with it. The subtle communication signals between you and your body start to disappear.

Without these messages, it's much harder to know when you're off balance. Your capacity to address your personal needs is diminished and this can lead to all sorts of problems. You overeat, you undereat, you become chronically stressed, you get burnt out. You become physically malnourished and emotionally drained. You experience binge urges, panic attacks and chronic pains. You feel empty, hungry for meaning, lonely, restless and somewhat lost.

It's like a circus tightrope walker. A tightrope walker relies on very small, subtle signals from his body to know if he is off balance or not. He is constantly tuning into his body, listening to his biofeedback and constantly adjusting in order to maintain his balance. This enables him to achieve the amazing feat of walking across a rope. But if those subtle signals from his body were to disappear the tightrope walker would come crashing to the ground. Think of yourself as that tightrope walker and that rope as your health. No body signals, no balance and off you fall.

In this stage of the program you are going to learn the art of BioBalancing™ so you can stay **in balance**. You will learn to nourish and balance your biological needs by paying attention to your biofeedback. By doing so you will stay at your healthy weight for life, binge free and you will know exactly when, how much and what to eat that is right for you. This is a process we have developed over 10 years working with clients who have binge eating issues.

THE 3 CORE PRINCIPLES OF BIOBALANCING™

BioBalancing™ has 3 core principles:

1. **Nourish**: Address your core needs (eat, sleep, relax, self-care, exercise etc)
2. **Observe**: Tune into your body sensations (your biofeedback) throughout the day
3. **Rebalance:** Figure out what you need to do/adjust/change to maintain balance.

Nourish, Observe and Rebalance. Three simple principles that can have a massive, lifelong, positive impact on your health and wellbeing. Let's explore them a little closer.

BioBalancing™ Principle 1: Nourish

This is all about nourishing your fundamental core needs. Think of this as addressing the fundamental requirements a human body needs to stay in balance.

Make sure that you:

- Eat enough nutritious balanced food
- Get enough sleep
- Nurture your needs
- Basically just look after yourself

If you are ever feeling off-balance the first thing you need to do is to question whether or not you are adequately nourishing your core needs. This principle is your bedrock, your foundation, your anchor for staying in balance. If you do not look after your core needs it is going to be impossible to stay in balance.

BioBalancing™ Principle 2: Observe

Via subtle feelings, sensations and feedback your body is constantly informing you of its current state. You can tap into this insight and knowledge by observing how you feel throughout the day. The more you practice the clearer and stronger the signals will become.

This may sound a little wishy-washy, but it's all backed up by science. The insula is the area in the brain that allows you to feel and sense the internal sensations of your own body (an ability known as interoception). Studies have shown that when you focus on becoming fully present in your own body the insula actually grows and becomes more complex. In other words, your brain becomes better at feeling what you're feeling. This is something scientific and measurable.

BioBalancing™ Principle 3: ReBalance

Over time as you start to observe your body, you will develop a 'base level' understanding of how your body feels normally. This puts you in much better position to notice when you're off-balance. You are better able to notice when you are feeling stressed, hungry, tired, emotional or have the early signs of a binge urge. Just like the tight rope walker you can then figure out what you need to do/adjust/change to get back in balance.

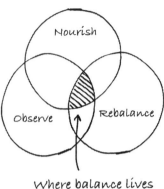

Where balance lives

BioBalancing in Action

So how do you apply the BioBalancing principles to your life? Simple, you just nourish, observe and rebalance throughout the day.

For example, by **observing** your body you may notice that you are feeling a bit stressed and sensitive. So you **rebalance** by ensuring you take some extra time to nourish and relax.

Perhaps you **observe** that you aren't feeling as fresh as usual. You examine whether you are properly **nourishing** your core needs and you realise that you've had a few too many late nights in a row. You are a little sleep deprived. So you **rebalance** by ensuring you get at least 7 hours sleep the next night.

You **observe** that you are feeling more hungry than usual, with more muscle fatigue. You realise that you have been working out more and that you should increase your food intake (**nourish**) to help your body heal (**rebalance**).

You **observe** some binge urges. You know that any binge urges are your body's way of telling you it is off-balance. You recognise that you're having a tough time at work and you are feeling emotionally vulnerable. You rebalance by taking extra "you" time.

By following these three simple principles you ensure you stay balanced and binge free.

KNOW WHEN AND HOW MUCH TO EAT

Let's explore how BioBalancing can help us figure out when and how much we should eat. We can do this by observing our hunger and satiety signals.

By far the most common reason for unnecessary weight gain in western culture is constant overeating. In our society, we ignore our hunger and fullness cues. If we continue to ignore our fullness cues, after a while they just fade away and we end up eating more than we need simply because we don't realize we're full.

Through BioBalancing you will learn to get back in touch with your hunger and fullness cues so you can eat an amount of food that's just right for you. Even if you eat a little too much, or not enough at a meal, that's perfectly okay. The next time you eat, your hunger levels will naturally adjust to take that into account. This helps you to avoid overeating (and undereating) and allows you to easily and happily maintain your natural, healthy weight for life.

―――

OBSERVING HUNGER

For a long time I didn't trust my hunger. I saw it as my enemy, something to be ignored, fought with and challenged. Yet to really make peace with my body and food I realised I needed to make peace with, listen to and understand my hunger. And you do too. Your hunger has a lot to teach you if you let it. Besides, this isn't as hard or scary as you might imagine. All you need to do is to simply start paying more attention to it. That's all.

How to do this

Throughout the day ask yourself, "How hungry am I and what does it feel like?". Drop your awareness into your body and then just make a mental note of what you observe. By asking this question repeatedly you start to build up a clear picture of what hunger feels like for you. Eventually tuning into your hunger will become a habit.

If you wish, rate your hunger level by using the Hunger Scale below:

The Hunger Scale:

1. Too hungry

2. Hungry

3. No particular feeling

4. Satisfied

5. Overly full

To stay in balance try to avoid becoming *too hungry* or *overly full*. Aim to eat when you are *hungry* and stop eating when you are *satisfied*.

What does my hunger feel like?

For most of us hunger can be described as an empty, irritating, insecure feeling. Some other physical signs of hunger include:

- Growling stomach
- Lightheadedness
- Difficulty concentrating
- Irritability
- Weakness and fatigue
- Headaches
- Nausea
- Feeling cold

"I can't feel any hunger!"

Recognizing subtle hunger cues can be challenging. You may only be used to experiencing hunger as extreme binge urges. This is very normal. Continue working on the seven keys and in time the sensations will return as your body becomes more balanced. A little patience is required here.

"I am not sure if I am hungry"

If you are not sure if you are really hungry apply the Zen10 technique. Wait 10 minutes and see how you feel afterwards. Real hunger pangs tend to continually reappear every 10 minutes or so. If your hunger pangs remain then you know that it is real hunger and that you should eat.

Rebalancing your hunger

If you feel the subtle sensations of hunger then you know this is a clear sign that you are hungry and that it's time to eat. By doing so you rebalance your hunger.

Avoid letting yourself get too hungry (too off-balance) as this can lead to poor food choices, anxious feelings and binge urges. If you are using the hunger scale to track your hunger you will want to eat before you reach "too hungry".

"Why does my hunger fluctuate so much from day to day?"

Hunger fluctuates all the time. You can be only slightly hungry one day, yet incredibly hungry the next. Your body is very complex and a lot of factors can affect your level of hunger, such as:

- Exercise and physical activity levels
- What you ate previously (your last meal, over the last day or over the last week)
- Genetics
- Muscle size
- Metabolism
- Amount and quality of sleep
- Mood and stress levels
- Hormonal cycles

Sometimes there are no obvious reasons for day-to-day hunger fluctuations, but we must accept that changes in hunger levels are normal. We've got to trust that our bodies know best. I know that for many binge eaters who haven't learned to trust their hunger, this can be scary. You may feel greedy or out of control, when you're really just hungry.

If you are a woman then you're probably already aware of the fact that you tend to experience an upsurge in binge urges and cravings for sugary, energy-dense foods in the days leading up to your period. However, as scary as this can be, research shows that there is a very straightforward explanation; your metabolism raises at this time and your body simply needs the extra fuel to restore balance.

Just keep on observing your hunger. In time you will start to make lots of mental connections between your hunger levels and lifestyle habits.

For example, you may notice how your stress level, exercise intensity or sleep quality impacts on your hunger levels.

BioBalancing™ Hunger Summary

Observe your hunger throughout the day. Ask yourself "how hungry am I and what does that feel like?". Avoid getting too hungry (off-balance) before eating. When you feel real hunger you should eat.

OBSERVING FULLNESS

It took me some time before I had any clear understanding of what proper satiety felt like. For a long time I under ate during my meals and over ate during my binges. I struggled to find the balance. But with practice and time I got it. And you will too. It is all part of the process of observing, learning and understanding your own body.

What does satiety feel like?

You are looking to feel a sense of satisfaction with eating. This isn't feeling overly full. It's more a feeling of being comfortably content. Not too heavy and not too light. As you eat you may notice how the food becomes less tasty and more bland. This is a clear sign that you are approaching satiety. Look out for a gentle, clear, satisfied sensation in the solar plexus (the area below your rib cage but above your stomach). Ideally you will still feel light, energetic and ready to move on with your day. This feeling indicates that you have accurately ate the right amount of food that is perfect for you. **You are perfectly in balance.**

If you are not sure if you are satisfied, pause, put your hand on your stomach and imagine the feeling of being comfortably full. Decide how much more food you think will be required to make you feel truly satisfied and then eat that amount. You may need to put more food on your plate or you may need to adjust your ratios of protein, fats and carbs to feel truly satisfied.

Pay attention whilst eating

Satiety is trickier to spot than hunger as it is much more subtle. Because of this it is important we **pay attention** whilst eating. If we are not paying attention we can easily miss the comfortably full sensation that tells you to stop eating.

A joint study conducted by Duke and Indiana State Universities revealed that binge eaters who participated in a nine-week program of mindful eating went from binge eating four times a week to just once a week. **Just by paying attention!**

When eating, turn off the T.V, put away your phone, put your book down and just focus on the food. Put your food on a plate and eat your food at a table (not standing up, or with your head halfway inside the fridge). For bonus points try lighting a candle, playing some relaxing music, or setting the table attractively.

As much as possible we want to avoid eating when stressed. When stressed, your sympathetic nervous system turns on and diverts blood away from your digestive system which slows digestion and turns down your digestive fire. If you're feeling a little tense before your meal, take 5 slow deep calm breaths.

Eat a little slower

It can take up to 20 minutes for any feelings of fullness and satiety to register. If you're eating meals much faster than this, it's very easy for you to overeat. You don't have to eat at a snail's pace, you just need to start eating your meals a little slower than usual. You can put your knife and fork down between bites. You can also take your time chewing your food. Many studies have found that properly chewing food does indeed reduce food intake. The longer you chew food, the more satiating it becomes. Digestion actually starts in the mouth, so the more work you do here, the less you'll have to do in your stomach.

Rebalancing satiety

We want to still feel balanced after eating. If we eat too much we can feel too full, too heavy, too-off balanced. So as soon as you notice that you are truly satisfied then stop eating. Put your knife and fork down and walk away from the table (or place your napkin on your plate if you're in a restaurant).

COACH CORNER

You can apply this principle to any snacks you eat. I will never forget the time I ate half a chocolate bar and decided to save the rest for later. It blew my mind. I'd always had such a tough time eating chocolate in a controlled way, it was typical for me to binge on extreme amounts of it, but there I was, happy and satisfied after eating just half a bar!

Catherine Liberty

"What if I think I've just eaten too much?"

Do not panic. This is very normal, so please don't worry. This is a skill and it takes practice. If you feel you have eaten too much, then make sure to stop eating and walk away from the table. Do not feel guilty about eating the extra food. Understand that if you overeat at one meal, your body will naturally self-correct and you will not feel so hungry at the next meal.

"I keep slipping back into a daydream when I'm eating"

This is totally normal. Most of us love to "zone-out" and daydream when we eat. Avoid getting frustrated if you find your mind continues to wander. Just gently bring your attention back to the act of eating. Do this as many times as you need to and over time you will naturally become more mindful and present during meals.

BioBalancing™ Satiety Summary

Observe and pay attention during meals. Eat slowly and stop eating when you feel comfortably satisfied. You want to feel balanced. Not too heavy and not too light. You will still feel, energetic and ready for the next activity.

 Use The Binge Code Food Journal to help track your hunger, satiety. Visit www.thebingecode.com/bonus.

BIOBALANCE YOUR FOOD CHOICES

I had to trust myself! Really??? Yes… really.

Years of abusing myself, undermining myself, ignoring my needs clearly wasn't working for me. That much was obvious. Wasn't it Albert Einstein who said that insanity is doing the same thing over and over again and expecting different results. It was time to do something different. I had to stop letting external outside forces dictate how I lived my life. No more diet plans or food rules. No more second guessing, ignoring or undermining my personal needs. It was MY life. I had to live it MY way. I had to acknowledge the fact that I knew best how to find the right balance for me. Sure I might stumble along my own path, but at least it was my own path.

Was I feeling confident? No. Of course not. But I took my lack of confidence as a clear sign that I was pushing myself into new territory. Bye bye comfort zone. Hello personal discovery.

In this chapter you are going to learn to use your gut instincts (your inner wisdom) to help you decide what to eat. You are going to learn to trust yourself.

You will learn to choose foods based on what you **feel like** eating and how that food **affects your balance**. This is a simple 2 step process.

1. Check-in with your gut to discover what you feel like eating (observe).
2. Ensure your food choice is adequately balanced (rebalance).

Let's explore these in a little more detail:

1. Check-in with your gut to discover what you feel like eating

To help you decide what to eat, begin by checking in with your gut. We've all had gut feelings. We've all "gone with our gut" to make a decision or felt "butterflies in our stomach". But did you know that your gut is smart? It's sometimes called the "second brain" and it's the only organ in the body besides the brain to have its own nervous system. At this point in time, even though the research is incomplete and complex, it's clear that the brain and gut are so intimately connected that it sometimes seems like one system, not two.

Drop your awareness into that region and notice if your gut is giving you a food preference. Spend a few moments there. Give your gut a little time to answer. You can even rest your hands on your stomach and take a few deep breaths. Try to imagine the taste of foods you might be hungry for and that you might find to be **most satisfying**. Let your body (not your mind, your emotions, or other people's diets) lead your food choice here. Try to let go of any preconceived notions or ideas of what you should or shouldn't have to eat and be open to accepting whatever signals your gut may give you.

Your gut may give you a clear preference for a specific food or just a general, vague idea. However, there will be lots of times when your gut doesn't indicate a clear preference. At these times it's best to choose foods that adhere to the Binge Code philosophy (i.e. wholefoods and a good balance of carbs, fats and proteins).

Why do we need to do this?

Knowing about nutrition isn't good enough. We put too much focus on nutritional rules and diet plans and we ignore what really works to meet our **own biological needs**. If we don't listen to our biological needs we can be easily led off-balance.

2. Ensure your food choice is adequately balanced

Now that you know what type of food your body is craving for, next ensure your food preference is adequately balanced. Here is a great question you can use.

Ask yourself **"Will this food satisfy me in a balanced way?"**.

If it is not balanced, figure out how you need to adjust your food preference to ensure that it is balanced. Perhaps your food choice is lacking fats and you may need to add an avocado or a few nuts. Perhaps you need to increase your protein intake by adding a boiled egg. Whatever you need to do to ensure you feel balanced, satisfied and content for at least a few hours.

For further insight, imagine eating the foods and consider how you will feel afterwards. Think back to when you ate those foods in the past. Did they knock you off balance or did you feel good after eating them? Were you hungry soon afterwards? Did you have any issues with the food? Use the knowledge gained from your personal experience to help guide your food choices.

Getting the balance right

If we put too much focus on what we think we SHOULD eat, we may miss out on foods that we REALLY want to eat and then end up feeling deprived. If we put too much focus on what we WANT to eat we may be drawn to foods that might not be adequately balanced, or might cause us to be too hungry too soon after eating.

It's like Goldilocks and the Three Bears. We want our porridge to be just right, so we feel happy, content, satisfied and balanced for two to three hours.

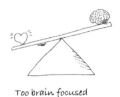

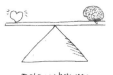

Too brain focused
Can lead to feelings of deprivation as you may not eat foods that you really want

Too heart focused
Can lead to hunger and cravings as you may eat food that is not adequatley balanced

Balance between heart & mind :)
Eat foods that make you feel satisfied and are adequately balanced

Boosting your BioBalancing™ skills

You are not always going to get this right. This is a skill and it takes practice. To become more comfortable with BioBalancing, start to **observe** your personal experience with eating food. An hour or two after eating check-in with yourself and **observe** how you feel.

You may notice:

- How the food feels in your stomach.
- If you feel satisfied or are you still hungry for more food.
- If you have any cravings for specific foods.
- Changes in your energy levels.
- Changes in your mood.

Do this regularly and overtime you will build up a mental library of different moods and physical feelings that result from different foods. Each time you eat something different you can add to your database of knowledge. These vital observations can be stored and used next time to help you make more effective choices.

If after eating a particular food you're feeling groggy, nauseous, or physically unwell then don't beat yourself up. Thank yourself for noticing that useful information. This does not mean eliminating that food altogether (remember, we're doing away with rules) it may simply mean not eating as much next time.

A real life example

Consider the scene: It's Monday morning. You're sitting at your desk preparing to eat the greek yogurt and fresh fruit you've packed for your mid-morning snack. But then your colleague gleefully brings in a tray of donuts for everyone and now you're conflicted. What do you choose? How do you make the choice?

Firstly ask yourself "**Will this food satisfy me in a balanced way**?"

If you feel that a donut will satisfy you in that moment and that it won't throw you off balance too much, then go ahead and eat it. It's very important to prevent feelings of deprivation. So opt for the donut, savour it and really try to enjoy it, guilt-free. It is perfectly normal and healthy to eat something that isn't necessarily the most nutritious choice if you feel it will satisfy you in that moment. BioBalanced eating is inclusive and non-restrictive. It does not assign moral values to foods.

If you're not sure, imagine eating the food and consider how you will feel afterwards. How did you feel the last time you ate a donut. Did you feel happy and satisfied? Or did it cause an energy slump?

Times when you may choose to not eat the donut include:

1. I'm not really in the mood for it.
2. I've been feeling out of balance recently. I'm feeling a bit wired and stressed. Getting back in balance is a big priority for me right now. So the donut's not worth it.
3. I'm full. No cravings. No thanks.
4. Last time I ate a donut, I felt a bit gross afterwards. So, no thanks.

Other options:

Why not choose to take the donut and save it for later? Wrapping it up and keep it for a snack (or a meal add-on) later that day can really help you to avoid feeling deprived in the moment. It can also help you to avoid eating the donut when you're not really hungry for it.

Alternatively, why not eat both? Eat a portion of your prepared snack together with a portion of the donut. This way you're getting **balance and satisfaction**. It's really a win-win situation. If you want to do this but you're afraid of losing control and eating too much, try to throw away any excess food before you start to eat, this way if urges to overeat or binge do arise, you won't have immediate access to the extra food.

COACH CORNER

Right now, it's all about making food choices that are right for you in the moment. Often, that can mean turning down sugary, processed foods for more balanced, nutritious options, but when you do this keep it straight in your mind - this is about feeling better, feeling balanced. It is never about depriving yourself in the ways you would if you were following a strict diet. There were many times when I turned down foods like this because my biofeedback taught me that I would only go on to experience more sugar cravings later in the day. But more often than not, I'd have both and I really recommend this balanced approach!

Catherine Liberty

Stay flexible and open to change

Our food choices and preferences can change a lot over time. The foods we find satisfying and balanced right now may not have the same effect six months from now. Environmental factors, pregnancy, change of exercise duration or type, illness and many other factors can stir up changes with our food choices. This is normal. Try to remain flexible and open to change.

Explore and discover (and maybe even have fun!)

Take a break from your old routines and food habits, try something new and really discover what makes you feel satisfied and content. If you have always eaten oatmeal for breakfast try mixing it up and having a breakfast of eggs, toast and avocado, it's an all-rounder. See what happens, check in and be mindful of your food thoughts, satiety and energy levels. See if you notice a difference. It may help to think of yourself as a scientist during this period, testing out different hypothesis to see the results. Ask yourself "what if I try that out?" and then see what happens.

BioBalanced Eating Summary

Nourish

- Ensure you address your core need for nourishment.
- Eat enough, balanced nutritious food spread throughout the day.

Observe

- Observe your hunger throughout the day.
- Pay attention and eat slowly during meals and notice when you feel comfortably satisfied.
- Check-in to your gut and figure out what type of foods it is asking for.

Rebalance

- Avoid getting too hungry (off-balance).
- Ask yourself "Will this food satisfy me in a balanced way?". Adjust your food preference to ensure that it is balanced so

you feel satisfied, nourished and cravings free for at least a few hours.

- Stop eating when you feel satisfied. You'll want to feel balanced. Not too heavy and not too light. You'll still feel energetic and ready for the next activity

BIOBALANCE YOUR LIFE

This is your life. This moment. Here and now. The place you really want to be is here and now. The person you really want to be is right here, right now. The best that life has to offer isn't somewhere else. In fact, life can only be lived right where you are, at this moment. But the question is… is your mind actually present here and now?

The reason I ask is because the act of BioBalancing is a very mindful skill. BioBalancing is like an anchor into the present moment. Each time you check-in with yourself you are being mindful. Each time you cater to your needs you are displaying the mindful traits of compassion and love. This can have a powerfully positive knock-on effect for the rest of your life.

This is how this works:

The more you practice BioBalancing, the more clarity and understanding you'll have of your internal emotional landscape. Your own motivations and drives become clearer to you. Your true needs and wants become apparent. Your core values become more defined. Not just in a conceptual way, but in a way that you can physically detect, moment by moment, throughout your day. You won't get some glaring flashing sign or signal, it's much subtler than that, just a general feeling of when something is "right" and when something is "wrong" for you. A sort of deep sense of wisdom. You'll just know, deep in your soul. Once you get a clearer indication of what makes you happy you can start to align your life accordingly to achieve more of it.

I believe this is the secret key to true happiness. It's not about getting more stuff, a bigger house or a fancier car. It's about you tapping into the real you and discovering what **really** makes you **truly fulfilled** and happy. It's what we all really want deep down. To live a happy life. To experience that true happiness that sinks deep into your bones and effects everything you do.

To do this, simply follow the 3 BioBalance principles:

1. **Nourish:** Ensure you are addressing your core needs.

2. **Observe:** Observe your emotional landscape within your body and discover what's really important to you.

3. **Rebalance:** Figure out what you need to do to achieve more of what you **really** want at a deeper level.

You know, recently I've become passionate about taking my family out for walks. I just love staring at the scenery, watching the grass, feeling the wind and just being amazed. That exuberance, that feeling of life, it's blissful. This is something I have discovered I really enjoy from tapping into my body sense.

My life has changed in so many positive ways since I started listening to my internal guidance system. That's not to say my life is all sunshine and roses, it still certainly has its fair share of challenges, but when you're really connected to the true you, when you're feeling balanced and when you nourish your core needs, life just flows a lot smoother. A profound shift occurs in how you feel, in how you interact with others, in your relationships, your sense of self, your productivity. Everything.

Balance NOT perfection

What you need to keep in mind is that we're striving for a **more balanced life**, not a perfect life (perfection doesn't exist and it's a sure-fire path to misery). The key word is "striving". We are never, ever, truly perfectly balanced. Like a tree blowing in the wind we need to allow ourselves to sway from side to side when the wind blows. Our life needs to be flexible, we need to be open to and accepting of whatever crops up in the present moment. Life can throw us a curveball at any moment and we need to be ready to accept that. The key is to really have **an attitude of always striving for balance** whilst becoming more accepting of unexpected changes and outcomes (this includes setbacks and relapses!).

So learn to trust your inner wisdom, your instincts, your body awareness. If it feels right for you, it is right for you. If it doesn't feel right, then change it. All the wisdom and knowledge you need is already there, inside you.

The great thing about BioBalancing is that it is a skill. It's something you can get better at throughout your life. It is a process of self-discovery in the truest sense. It's a wonderful journey of self-exploration and it helps to strengthen, nurture and enhance the most important relationship in your life: **The one you have with yourself.**

BIOBALANCE BOOSTER

This is a great tool we can use to help boost our skills with BioBalancing. It will help us to get out of our head and back in touch with our body. It was pioneered by a psychologist called Dr Peter Levine to help patients overcoming trauma and it's all about tapping into the felt sense.

To start doing this, simply drop your awareness into your body and notice what you feel. You may ask yourself, *"How does my body feel?"*. Just notice whatever it is you feel in this moment. Do you feel anything on the surface of your skin, like clothing, pressure or a breeze? Can you feel any parts of you touching other parts? Can you feel any tension, movement, space or warmth inside you? Do you notice any strong emotions or feelings?

Most of the time you will feel a vague, fuzzy, complex and ever changing sensation. At times it may be clear and at times it may be undefined. Most of the time it can be hard to put a label on exactly what you are feeling; as though it doesn't fit easily into a simple box or category. If you cannot put a label on what you're feeling, that's okay. I suggest you don't try. Just experience the sensation as it is. The idea here is to **feel**, not to think or analyze.

"How does my body feel?"

This is actually a very simple form of meditation. By doing this we are exploring our innate sense of aliveness, vitality and energy that exists moment to moment and that otherwise goes unnoticed. We're getting to really understand and know what it feels like to be us. In a way, this is a personal journey of self-exploration in the truest sense.

Tuning in to your felt senses (I call this a Check-in) is a skill and like all skills it takes a little practice. Think of this exercise in the same way you would doing reps in the gym. The more you practice, the stronger your body awareness muscle becomes. It only takes a few moments to do, so I would recommend getting into the habit of doing this multiple times each day. When driving the car, when practicing the "I love myself" mantra, when talking to someone, whenever you experience an intense emotion, even during a binge episode.

If you haven't been aware of your body sensations for a long time it can initially feel a little uncomfortable or awkward. You may even feel some anxiety and fear. Think about it like this: Have you ever bumped into an old, long lost friend? Someone you haven't seen in years. Initially it can be a little awkward as you get to know each other again. But it doesn't take long before you get back into the old groove and become the best of buddies again. Similarly, as you practice, it won't take long before you really connect and feel much more comfortable with your body awareness.

I've developed this habit so much now that there is a part of my mind that is nearly always aware of how my body is feeling at any given moment. I honestly cannot describe the numerous ways this has dramatically improved my life over the years.

As you continue to Check-in, you'll begin to discover who you really are, deep down, underneath all that baggage that life tends to throw on top of us. Don't worry if you don't feel anything magical at first. Most people won't. Just keep practicing. Keep bringing your attention to your body awareness and with time, you'll start to learn how your body communicates with you. The exploration of how you feel at any given moment is a lifelong journey of discovery and it will change your life for the better, **that's a certainty.**

If you wish to make this more formal, you can do a simple, 3-minute Check-in exercise twice a day. Do this at least once each morning and at least once in the evening:

3-Minute Check-in Technique

This should take you roughly three minutes to do.

Start by deliberately adopting an erect and dignified sitting posture and drop your awareness and attention into your body. Ask yourself, "How does my body feel?"

Then, do a body scan:

Start with your feet. Notice the feeling of your feet touching the floor.

Start to move your awareness up your body.

Become aware of your legs resting against the chair.

Notice any sensations such as pressure, pulsing, heaviness, lightness.

Move up towards your hips. Feel the weight on your bones where you sit.

Bring your attention into your stomach area.

Notice the sensation of your back resting on the chair.

Notice your arms and hands.

Move up to your neck and shoulders.

Finally, become aware of your face and head.

Then place your awareness gently inside your body. Rest your awareness inside your body as a whole. Just let yourself notice what you sense to build up a stronger picture of how your body feels. Sit here for roughly one minute noticing whatever it is you notice. You can stop after a minute or you can continue with this technique for as long as you wish.

If you find it challenging to feel anything I would suggest gently twitching your muscles, twitch your toes, your legs, your fingers. This can help your mind to recognize the different body sensations that are present.

You may wish to do this practice while listening to the Binge Code Check-in Audio (download from www.thebingecode.com/bonus), at least the first few times that you do it. Then feel free to do it on your own, silently guiding your own practice for about three minutes.

Visit   www.thebingecode.com/bonus   to download the 3 Minute Check-in audio.

BIOBALANCE YOUR EMOTIONS (ADVANCED)

We can use BioBalancing to help your emotions recalibrate so you feel more in balance. You can do this by learning to observe uncomfortable feelings and emotions. This is an advanced practice of BioBalancing, so don't stress if you find this too challenging to begin with. Down the line, when you feel more comfortable with BioBalancing, this is something you definitely want to incorporate.

Balancing your emotions

I know that feeling painful emotions, not surprisingly, can be painful. This is why so many of us are tempted to binge on food to suppress and numb these feelings. It amazes me how many of my clients find it difficult to just be with themselves. If they sat for even a few moments they would get uncomfortable and then have to do something to distract themselves from how they felt. Their entire life is set up all day long to stop them from ever having to feel even a little bit of discomfort or unease. But, as we know, this strategy is not very helpful in the long term. Avoiding emotions becomes a prison because the more you avoid, the weaker you feel, the more your coping skills diminish and the more it shrinks your life.

We are all human, we all feel a range of emotions, pleasant and unpleasant. At times we all feel insecure, not good enough, sad, unloved, this is a normal part of being human. These are normal, natural emotions. It is okay to feel this way. It is not wrong. These emotions do not define our worth. We don't need to suppress or hide or deny them. Instead we need to recognize these emotions and respectfully acknowledge them. Your feelings belong to you and it is okay to let yourself feel them. They are an important part of your very being.

So instead of trying to block out every uncomfortable emotion an alternative is to simply accept and observe your emotions. Observing your emotions simply means allowing them to be, resisting the urge to get rid of the pain and not judging yourself for having these feelings.

This is helpful for many reasons. When you observe an emotion:

- You don't have to spend all your energy pushing the emotion away or fighting it.
- You allow yourself to feel the emotion, you start to learn about the qualities of the emotion, become familiar with it and eventually become skilled in its management.
- You will realize that although not fun, experiencing negative emotions takes less effort than bingeing on food in an attempt to avoid them.
- Finally, when you accept a negative emotion, it is usually nowhere near as destructive, uncomfortable or challenging as you may have imagined. Put simply, it doesn't feel so bad.

Think of all the uncomfortable emotions that you automatically respond to with a binge without even a moment's consideration. By giving emotions some space to be and exist you start to gain some measure of control. Rather than simply reacting to the emotion, you begin to cultivate a space between stimulus and response, you gain the ability to choose whether to respond to an emotional urge or not. This is the essence of emotional intelligence.

What you need to do

If you notice you are experiencing an uncomfortable feeling, stop for a moment. Take a deep breath and then just **observe the feeling**. Don't inhibit it, suppress it, ignore it or try to conquer it. Just be with it with an attitude of open curiosity and acceptance.

The key word here is **acceptance**. Acceptance simply means being aware of your emotions and accepting them for what they are right now, knowing that they won't last. It's about relaxing and **letting go of all resistance** to any discomfort you may feel, whether that resistance is mental or physical. **Let the discomfort be there**, accept it, don't try to change or control it. Physically relax around it as much as possible. Give it all the room in the world to be itself. Let everything just be the way it is right now, even if that's a little scary and uncomfortable. Really focus on the acceptance aspect of it.

Fighting against your emotions all the time and bingeing to block them out, only creates more stress and discomfort in your life. Let go of the fight. End the war. Drop the resistance and **let the emotions flow through** you as a river flows downstream.

When we sit with an emotion there is no need to wallow in the experience. We don't need to dwell on the situation and ruminate about the details. Accepting emotions does not mean that you resign yourself to always feeling terrible or wallowing in pain. It also doesn't mean that you hold on to painful emotions or try to push yourself to experience emotional pain. Sometimes when we feel a very painful emotion, like anger or a deep grief, we hold onto it, or we intensify it, making it stronger or bigger, in our efforts to deal with it or to give it our full attention. Try not to do this. **Just let it be however it is**. Like a cloud floating in the sky, just let it do its own thing. This can result in a lessening of the pain.

Emotions are always in a state of flux, always changing. And by accepting and allowing the emotion you allow it to change, to morph and eventually move on. Emotions are fleeting and usually go away or change within seconds or minutes if you let them run their course.

You can think of the emotion as a wave, coming and going. Your task is simply to allow this current wave to be and to witness, with patience, as it continuously changes form and eventually disappears. Drop your awareness into your body and just notice how your body is feeling at this moment. This is what I like to do and it can be so interesting to notice how different emotions affect your body in their own unique ways.

Although you might feel uncomfortable, you don't have to fear the discomfort. Really emotions are simply bodily sensations. That's all. Bingeing on food over the years has rocked your confidence in your ability to handle uncomfortable emotions. But as you observe, in time you will notice that you can handle them.

You don't have to be critical of yourself for feeling this way either. Feeling bad doesn't always mean that there's something wrong with you, or that you did something wrong. Anger, fear and sadness are all painful emotions, but they are not bad. Everyone has them and they are just as valid as happy emotions. Rather than getting angry, anxious or depressed about the uncomfortable feelings we're having, let go of the tendency to explain or get rid of them. Just accept that the way you feel is the way you feel. Every feeling is part of the experience of life. In fact, the idea that we're supposed to be happy all of the time is a relatively new concept, it is simply not true. Feeling happy all of the time would take away the true moments of happiness that are to be treasured in life.

Research shows that we have very little control over our emotions. They are simply happening, like your heartbeat or your breathing, so it really does make sense to let go of the struggle of trying to control them.

Real growth and learning happens when we challenge ourselves, when we push beyond our comfort levels. So, know that this isn't about avoiding discomfort, but instead accepting it as part of the journey to change. When you accept the presence of negative emotions in your life they lose a lot of their power over you. You reduce that huge anxious reaction that happens when you're feeling lonely, unloved, overwhelmed, etc. And in doing so you reduce the need to immediately act on numbing or escaping from those feelings.

COACH CORNER

I remember reading about the importance of acceptance and things like "embracing the pain" and I'll be honest with you, back then, I thought it was the stupidest thing I'd ever heard. Why would anyone want to accept misery? Why would anyone want to accept that it was very possible they were going to feel urges to binge that day? Why would anyone accept the pain and confusion life throws their way? But eventually I caved in and decided to see what all the fuss was about. I felt so stupid at first trying to welcome emotions that hurt me because I just wanted to run away and hide instead. At first I remember everything hurting so much. There would be days, a lot of days actually, where I would just sit and cry, I was a total mess, but it was the only thing I could do because it all just felt like it was too much, you know?

Slowly things did change. After a short time, I noticed that I wasn't really having such a bad experience handling emotions anymore. I found that when I had a negative emotion or experienced a challenging day I wasn't automatically freaking out or going into panic mode. Instead I was sitting there, still feeling awful, but knowing I would be okay because I'd expected to be challenged and to feel that bad. It's hard to explain exactly just how amazing this kind of strategy can be for breaking free from binge eating and really for life. I think you can only really get it when you've practiced it a good few times, perhaps over a couple of weeks. It is going to feel scary and so unnatural at first, but I promise you that it is going to change absolutely everything for you in the long run.

Catherine Liberty

FINAL THOUGHTS

Congratulations! You made it through. Well done!

You've just given yourself the tools you need to break free from binge eating **forever**. Now, you just need to go forward and apply The Binge Code principles to your life.

I know we covered a LOT in this book, but really it all comes down to three simple words. Nourish, observe and rebalance. At the end of the day that is all you need to keep in mind. If you are feeling off-balance just ask yourself, "Am I nourishing my core needs? Am I observing how I feel throughout the day? And from my observations what do I need to do to rebalance?". That's it. That is the core of the Binge Code program. Three simple words that can have a massive, lifelong, positive impact on your health, happiness and wellbeing.

So, take a moment to imagine yourself one year from now, free from binge eating. Imagine your ideal day, what does it look like? How do you feel? Imagine some of the really fun and enjoyable things you'll do now you're free from binge eating. See yourself handling stressful situations calmly without turning to food. It feels good, doesn't it? This can be your future now. **You can have hope.**

Finally, never, ever, doubt that you can beat this. You can. You do not have to spend the rest of your life as a slave to food. We've helped thousands of people over the past 10 years with many suffering over 20, 30 and even 40 years with eating issues. Yet with determination, patience and commitment they did. They overcame this. You can do it too. You can be free. Really commit to the program and you will see the results!

This is my life's passion and it's been an honor to share it with you. Thank you so much for reading The Binge Code and spending time with me.

In health and love,

Ali

BE PERSONALLY COACHED THROUGH THE BINGE CODE PROGRAM

S uccess is easier when you have someone who's supporting you, guiding you, keeping you on track – every step of the way.

With this in mind we offer a coaching program for anyone looking for one-on-one support and guidance to overcome binge eating. All of our coaches have recovered from binge eating, so you'll be sharing your journey with someone who truly understands what you're going through. Once you've signed up you'll be assigned your own personal coach to work with. Gently, at a pace that is right for you, your coach will support and guide you step-by-step to binge freedom.

Visit: www.heal-ed.com to learn more about working with a certified coach to overcome binge eating.

CAN YOU DO ME A SMALL FAVOR?

My husband and I created this book out of a passion to help as many people as possible. The problem is that as companies go, we are very small. The Binge Code is a self-published book and does not have the marketing resources of a big publishing company.

If, like so many others, you've enjoyed the book I would greatly appreciate it if you could do me a small (yet big) favor and write an honest review of the book on our Amazon page. These reviews make a HUGE difference in reassuring others that this book is the real deal. Your review could be the very thing that propels others to take action and finally break free from binge eating.

I'm not looking for anything over the top, unbelievable or fabricated but instead something that is real and based on what you've read/experienced from the book. Also, you can use a pen name or be anonymous when you write an Amazon review.

It's a small favor but it will make a big difference to us. It would be greatly appreciated!

———

P.S. I wish you the best of luck on your incredible journey!

Ali ☺

Made in the USA
San Bernardino, CA
24 March 2018